Praise for Sharon Stone's

The Beauty of Living Twice

"*The Beauty of Living Twice* is far from the glitzy account of Hollywood that readers might expect. Instead, it shows a woman who's spent the majority of her years in the public eye seizing the opportunity to tell her story entirely on her own terms."
—*Time*

"[Stone] definitely has her own voice, and a strong one. . . . After unfathomable trauma and pain and loss and disaster, she's still standing, sharing this story from her own perspective, and now looking ahead to a path of her own making. There's real beauty in living like that."
—*Entertainment Weekly*

"Stone is a strong portraitist of the instant in time, and aware that stardom, like identity, is mostly a phenomenon of the memory."
—*The New Republic*

"While the actress takes a trip down memory lane throughout her memoir, she also takes readers on her journey to finding contentment and healing both physically and mentally."
—*The Hollywood Reporter*

"[A] powerhouse memoir. . . . Deeply compelling and re-defining."
—*Booklist*

Sharon Stone

The Beauty of Living Twice

Sharon Stone is an actress, human rights activist, artist, mother, daughter, sister, and writer. She has been honored with a Nobel Peace Summit Award, a Harvard Humanitarian Award, a Human Rights Campaign Humanitarian Award, and an Einstein Spirit Award, as well as many other accolades. She currently lives in Los Angeles with her family.

The Beauty of Living Twice

Sharon Stone

VINTAGE BOOKS
A Division of Penguin Random House LLC
New York

FIRST VINTAGE BOOKS EDITION, MARCH 2022

Copyright © 2021 by Sharon Stone

All rights reserved. Published in the United States by Vintage Books,
a division of Penguin Random House LLC, New York, and distributed in
Canada by Penguin Random House Canada Limited, Toronto. Originally
published in hardcover in the United States by Alfred A. Knopf,
a division of Penguin Random House LLC, New York, in 2021.

Vintage and colophon are registered trademarks of
Penguin Random House LLC.

Grateful acknowledgment is made to Harvard University Press for
permission to reprint an excerpt of "Because I could not stop for Death"
from *The Poems of Emily Dickinson: Reading Edition*, edited by Ralph W.
Franklin, Cambridge, Mass.: The Belknap Press of Harvard University Press,
copyright © 1998, 1999 by the President and Fellows of Harvard College.
Copyright © 1951, 1955 and copyright renewed 1979, 1983 by the President
and Fellows of Harvard College. Copyright © 1914, 1918, 1919, 1924,
1929, 1930, 1932, 1935, 1937, 1942 by Martha Dickinson Bianchi.
Copyright © 1952, 1957, 1958, 1963, 1965 by Mary L. Hampson.

The Library of Congress has cataloged the Knopf edition as follows:
Name: Stone, Sharon, author.
Title: The beauty of living twice / Sharon Stone.
Description: First edition. | New York : Alfred A. Knopf, 2021.
Identifiers: LCCN 2019954032
LC record available at https://lccn.loc.gov/2019954032

Vintage Books Trade Paperback ISBN: 978-0-525-56726-4
eBook ISBN: 978-0-525-65677-7

Author photograph © Michael Muller
Book design by M. Kristen Bearse

www.vintagebooks.com

Printed in the United States of America
10 9 8 7 6 5 4 3 2 1

For my mother

Because I could not stop for Death—
He kindly stopped for me—
The Carriage held but just Ourselves—
And Immortality.

We slowly drove—He knew no haste
And I had put away
My labor and my leisure too,
For His Civility—

—Emily Dickinson,
"Because I could not stop for Death"

Contents

Contents

The Beauty of Living Twice

Death Becomes Me

I opened my eyes, and there he was standing over me, just inches from my face. A stranger looking at me with so much kindness that I was sure I was going to die. He was stroking my head, my hair; God, he was handsome. I wished he were someone who loved me instead of someone whose next words were "You're bleeding into your brain."

He stood there gently touching my head and I just lay there knowing that no one in the room loved me. Knowing it in my guts—not needing my bleeding brain to be aware of the ridiculous slap-down of my now-immobilized life. It was late September 2001. I was in the ER at the California Pacific Medical Center in San Francisco. I asked Dr. Handsome, "Will I lose my ability to speak?" He said it's possible. I wanted a phone. I needed to call my mom and my sister. They needed to hear this from me while I could still tell them myself. The doctor squeezed my hand in his. I realized he was doing his darndest to fill in with that special kind of love that comes when someone pursues the vocation that they were meant to, if only for moments like this. I learned a lot from him.

I called my sister, Kelly, first. She was as she always is: the most magnificent person I know. She is kinder to others than she is to herself, naïve in her gentleness. Then I called my mom, a more difficult conversation for me, since I didn't know if she liked me very much. Here I was, dying and insecure all at the same time. She was gardening outside in her yard on top of a mountain in Pennsylvania. She fell apart.

It's important to consider that Dot falls apart over radio commercials, so I waited, because, well, I knew she would pull it together. Despite the distance between us, she and my dad arrived in under twenty-four hours. She ran into the hospital still in her shorts, covered in gardening mud, dirt under her nails and fear on her face. Years of uncertainty and miscommunication between us fell away in a look. As I lay there knowing that I could die at any second, she stroked my face with her dusty hand and I suddenly felt that my mother loved me. Bit by bit.

My father stood beside her like a bull looking to charge.

I called my best friend of more than twenty years, Mimi, and said what we always said when the news was exceptionally good or bad: "You'd better sit down." I could hear her sharp inhale. I said, "I might die and you are the only one I can tell the truth to because somebody needs to take care of everyone and it's not going to be me. I'm bleeding into my brain. They don't know why."

She said, "Oh, shit."

I said, "There is a very good-looking doctor here, and sadly I might not be able to flirt with him."

She was trying not to cry as she whispered, "Oh, honey, I'm on the next plane." As I knew she would be.

Then came the silence again. Echoing off the emergency room tiles and hitting my newly broken heart. I remember feeling something between scared and fascinated that no one was running around yelling, *"STAT STAT!"* like they do on TV. There was a stunning lack of urgency and movement. The doctor—yeah, that one—told me an ambulance was coming to transport me to another hospital, Moffitt-Long, which was renowned for neurological issues, and that they would take special care of me.

God, that really made me feel bad. There are just times when getting special care can be such a downer. This is not like floor seats at a Laker game or getting the table by the window at your favorite restaurant. Privileges. Fame. Shit.

It was then that I suddenly felt everything moving strangely, as if the film of my life were moving through a camera backward. Fast. I started to experience a feeling of falling, and then as though something were overtaking me, body and soul, followed by this tremendous, luminous, uplifting whiteout pulling me right out of my body and into a familiar brilliant other body of . . . knowing?

The light was so luminous. It was so . . . mystical. I wanted to know it. I wanted to immerse myself. Their faces were not just familiar. They were transcendent. Some of them had not been gone for long. I had cared for some of them until the end of this life. They were my closest friends, Caroline, Tony Duquette, Manuel. I had missed them so much. I felt so cold in the room

I was coming from. They were so warm, so happy, so welcoming. Without their saying a word, I understood everything they were telling me about why we are safe, why we should not be afraid: because we are surrounded by love. That in fact we *are* love.

Suddenly I felt like I had been kicked in the middle of my chest by a mule, the impact was so harsh, and, astoundingly, I was awake and back in the emergency room. I had made a choice. I took the kind of gasp you take when you are underwater far too long. I sat up; the light was blinding. All I could see was Dr. Handsome, standing back, observing me.

I had to pee so badly, but as I turned to get off the gurney, I was so high up, like an Alice in a Wonderland of white and stainless steel.

"What do you need?" the doctor said.

"Bathroom."

"There."

I slipped far, farther down onto the cool tiles, and felt like I floated to the toilet and peed for a long time, wandering back to where the doctor lifted me up like the feather I had become.

The last few years, throughout the late nineties, I had been chasing a love I didn't have. A love that I thought did, but didn't, belong to me. I chased literally—leaving Hollywood and moving to Northern California—figuratively, and spiritually: always trying to be something more, something that would be the thing that would bring me closer to understanding how to be better at life, better at love and loving. I was watching my own life, and suddenly it ran out right in front of me.

Suddenly, one fine, pretty afternoon, all of my questions were more than answered. Without gauze or haze or pretense: all of those efforts failed. The facts were just that: I was not loved, not wanted; I was less than.

In my fine and decent desire to be something more than I had been before, something I thought might be more real, I had failed. I had done everything I could think of, and nothing was the correct thing, nothing the right action. I thought at that time that if I kept doing what I thought was the correct and spiritually elegant thing to do, the thing I longed for would open to me. It did not. I had simply made bad choices. Uninformed choices. Spiritually impoverished choices. I had let the core me go in order to be "more." I thought I wasn't enough. I couldn't wife it away.

I was ignorant of the fact that I was not in the correct place for me or that I could leave, because, per usual, I wanted to be good at this. I wanted to do what I said. Even if I had made a mistake, I would carry it through, I would figure it out.

Until this time and this moment, when I had reached too far, wanted too much, I accepted what I shouldn't have, made deals with myself in an effort to figure out why I had given up so much for so little. Because I was a woman who had made it, very few people personally valued me for what I had done, what I had made of myself. It made it so much easier to give it away. After all, what was I? An actress? A fundraiser? Did I matter? Was the assessment of me true? Was I not really worth as much as a man with the same accomplishments?

I had grown up with parents who loved each other more than they were interested in their kids. Parents who we would find necking on the sofa when we came in from playing. I grew up with parents who still danced in the yard after fifty years of marriage, as if they were alone. I was not aware that there were people who just didn't love their spouses. I believed that even divorced people struggled with those big decisions. I was swimming in quicksand, losing all points of reference. I can tell you this: when I failed at the thing I left everything behind for—the thing I saw growing up, the real kind of love that matters—I had nothing left within to find *me*.

Weighed down by this new knowledge, this failure, I'd walked down the hall and into the TV room, past the sofas and toward the window, wanting to look out at the garden, where I had buried the ultrasound pictures of my miscarried children under the magnolia saplings (ones that would bloom with no scent), which seemed to be doing so well. Without warning, it was as if Zeus himself hurled a bolt of lightning directly under the back right-hand side of my head. I was airborne, flying over the back of the sofa, smashing into the coffee table, telephone, tablets, pens, papers, remotes, pillows, the sofas themselves going this way and that as my head bounced off the floor, bearing the brunt of my fall.

Haunted by memories, I lay there for what seemed a long time, time itself floating by while I was fascinated with the fibers in the rug, the lack of color in the room, and ultimately grateful for my aloneness. I think I slept there, or blacked out there.

Thankfully, there was a group of three young, local San Francisco–based Irish nannies who rotated coming in to help with my son, Roan, who I had only recently adopted, and who was very young at the time, just a wee babe. While deliriously happy to finally become a parent, already having lost three five-and-a-half-month pregnancies, I was old to be a new mom, already past forty, and sure I didn't know much of anything at all about parenting.

During the next few days, I wandered. At some point I got into my convertible and attempted to drive myself to the hospital. I had no idea where I was, and found myself at a stop sign, my right foot totally numb, the numbness creeping up my leg, as I looked up at the trees, heard words from the radio, thought, *Oh, I must have anthrax poisoning,* and felt tears running down my face, as this was just two weeks after 9/11. Fortunately someone pulled up beside me and offered to help me, guiding me home and taking me into my house. Where I just sat at the dining room table, telling our nanny I had a terrible pain in my head. She told me to take some aspirin, which may have saved my life.

The next morning I started to lose body temperature. I took a down comforter into the yard and tried to feel the sun. I couldn't get warm. I went upstairs and lay on my heated bathroom floor. The phone rang; someone stepped over me. I was holding a space outside and above my head where I thought the pain was, talking to myself while crying and moaning.

Thankfully, the speakerphone was on; it was Mimi. I tried to holler but croaked out instead, "Mimi, help me."

She insisted an ambulance be called.

Instead there was a call to my gynecologist; I guess that's

what some people always think is wrong with women: "Must be her lady parts."

My gynecologist heard me moaning and said to take my blood pressure, while she stayed on the line. We had one of those cuffs, and a defibrillator, as everyone in my house, including my staff and children, gets CPR and rescue training regularly, and stays up to date. My blood pressure was over the moon, both figures high in the hundreds. My doctor said we had a few minutes to get me to the hospital, which was just down the street, making clear that she would be standing outside waiting. She had been my attending doctor for my miscarriages and knew the fragility of my situation.

I was stuffed into our truck, my legs not really following my thoughts any longer. I slumped against the passenger door in the front seat. When we got to the California Pacific Medical Center, the burly attendant opened the door and I fell out upside down and backward into his warm and strong arms and passed out. I had made it. I let go. Somehow I had hung on until I fell into safety's arms.

They hustled me inside and onto a gurney, and immediately put me into a CAT scan machine, the noise so loud it was as if someone were hammering my mind from the inside out.

After I first woke up, Dr. Handsome told me the transfer ambulance had arrived. "They have everything you need at the other hospital," he said, and gave me an encouraging smile. Two young men picked me up and moved me onto another portable gurney and I passed out yet again. As they were putting me into the ambulance, that gurney's wheel hit the bottom of the truck and stirred me. I opened my eyes into the bright sunlight and saw a paramedic with white light surrounding him and wasn't sure if I was still alive as I passed out again.

I woke up in Moffitt-Long's neurological ICU. There were no rooms, just a nurses' central unit with beds in a circle around it, each one on a scale to measure our body weight and mass, curtains in between and in front of us. Lots of machines and hoses—it looked like a Fritz Lang movie. The sounds and lights of all those machines haven't left me still. They are wrapped up with the memory of the televisions hanging from the ceiling, still playing the endless images of the planes flying into the Twin Towers and the Pentagon. I took it in.

The next day I came to as I was being wheeled down the hall by a young male orderly. I asked where he was taking me.

"To the operating theater."

"For what?" I began to panic some more; this panic thing was starting to become more and more my full-time state of being.

"For exploratory brain surgery."

"But no one talked to me about it."

"Oh, yeah, the papers were signed—you're all good."

I asked him to stop for a second; I needed a minute to absorb all of this. But he told me that we didn't have time or we would lose the room. I could not get him to stop or call the doctor to help me in any way. So I did what I could: I gathered myself and stood up on that moving gurney. Which took every last bit of might, of strength, I had left.

Nurses and other hospital personnel came running. "She doesn't want to go to the surgery room," the orderly announced. A nurse came and asked me why, and I told her that I had been signed up for exploratory brain surgery without my knowledge or consent and with no discussion of what that could or would mean. The nurse said she would get the doctor.

He came running, white coat flapping, and told me to lie down and do what I was told. A fine hello, I have to say. He told us all that someone had signed all of the papers and we were well under way. He showed us all proudly that he was holding a fax from *People* magazine and said he had just spoken to them, told them of the situation, and he knew exactly what to do. (Ultimately, he had given them an incorrect diagnosis, which they ran.) He held it like a talisman, as if because it was written, it was true. Which it wasn't, by the way. Oh, if only he had been right.

I looked at the nurse, who stared at me with the same sense of incredulity, like, *This doctor is a jackass of astonishing proportions.* I realized that, brain bleed or not, this was a mess that I had to handle—now.

Still standing, ass out of my gown on the gurney, not giving up any ground, I turned to the doctor and said, "You're fired."

He said, "What? You can't fire me!" and the nurse said, "Doctor, I'm afraid she just did," and directed the orderly to take me back to my room.

That quick-thinking nurse saved my life. She was a pretty, blond fifty-something woman who I later realized was not dissimilar to someone I would get to be simply because she had the courage to be brave and true for me. To do her job with the authority and knowledge that she was the one to make that call, she stood in her dignity.

By now my entire family had rushed to the neurological unit: my mother, my father, my sister, and my brothers, Mike and Patrick. They were shocked and confused, as they had been led to believe that I was "sleeping and shouldn't be disturbed," not that I had been signed up for exploratory brain surgery without anyone being consulted.

My room became a free-for-all. Tempers were out of control. The just-fired doctor was still holding his *People* magazine fax. My older brother, Mike, wanted a fistfight; Kelly, who is a nurse, wanted medical facts; my friends who had arrived were like sentries, keeping the wrong people out and the right people in.

My friend Donna Chavous was there. Chavous and I had been through all kinds of hellcat endeavors in the past, including the day I became famous. We were at a movie and came out afterward and the whole theater of people was just hanging out in front and didn't leave. We slowly came to realize they were looking at us. Chavous whispered, "Run," to me and we did; we ran like thieves in the night, and yes, they all ran after us. We ran and ran across streets of moving cars, into a restaurant, into its kitchen, and slid under its chef's cutting table. The owner, having locked the front door behind us, leaned down and asked us what he could do for us. Chavous got tequila, I got a martini. The owner, knowing better than we did what was happening, asked us where our car was and got a waiter to go and get it and helped us to get out amid the frenzy and get home. Chavous and I had been martial arts partners, always racing each other in our cars while talking on our speakerphones, getting to the dojo late and doing push-ups on our knuckles to be allowed entrance. Yes, always pushing it, and having a ball. We always took care of each other.

Now she stayed for the entire time, days and nights, sleeping in a window seat at the hospital. Just to be sure.

My mother was determined no one was going to . . . well, as she would say, "fuck with my kid." She had had it. This was "too goddamn far." She was scared. Scared to stillness, scared beyond her rage, beyond her humor, beyond all telling. So she sat, outside the curtain. There, she sat. Purse on her lap. Tight-lipped, fierce, immobile, strong, and brittle. She guarded that spot and no one, but *no one,* was getting to me again until I knew and agreed.

I asked the fired flapping doctor to explain the steps of the proposed brain surgery to me. He was profoundly offended, still waving his fax, his fifteen minutes. He felt we didn't have the time and believed I really didn't need to know. I felt I really did. I felt I deserved knowledge about what this potential brain surgery would mean for me. Go figure.

"You shave my head and then cut the first layer of skin. Do you fold it back or remove it? Then the bone, do you remove it? Where do you put it? We are in earthquake country; does it go on a tray or in a sterile box? Then what? How large of a section of my head will you remove? Will you cut through the nerves?"

I have always been a thorough asker of questions. I made my inquiries in a slow, thoughtful panic that seemed quite logical to me. He was impatient, irritated, and seemed to think my questions were trivial and a waste of his time. I thought it was reasonable to spend ten minutes finding out where my brain would be during and after this surgery. He thought I was a nag. I realized I had fired the right guy.

The hospital then sent me a group of extraordinary men, a team of research doctors from the neurological unit, who talked to me about all of my options. They calmly told me that there was another neurosurgeon, but that he wasn't there that day. I asked if we could get him on the phone. They did. The lead guy in this group, Dr. Michael Lawton, explained that going with the neurosurgeon required waiting another day, as he had to fly in. I tried to get the doctors to talk odds, percentages with me. What could happen? How much more would I bleed into my brain waiting these twenty-four hours? How much damage could that cause? Could I die or just lose some senses? If so, which? Would it be reparable? There is so little known about these issues that at the best of times the answers are vague, even when your brain isn't bleeding, even when you aren't terrified. I chose to wait for him.

The next morning that brilliant neurosurgeon walked into my life. He talked to me and my family about a relatively new process of using a camera that would go into my femoral artery at the top of the leg and the front of the pelvis. That camera would go all the way through my body and up into my head and look around.

That felt so much better than half of my head on a tray. So that's what we did. But they did not find the cause of the bleeding.

Not too long before this fiasco I had endured another one. I had had a breast exam, only to have that doctor call me and say he needed to come out to the house to talk to me.

This is never great news. I spent that day preparing myself for a drive into a brick wall. Of course he said there was a tumor, a large one, one he thought would be malignant, one he thought must come out, one they would look at while I was out to determine how much more they might need to take. I responded with the calm I had prepared all day to have: "Hey, if it's cancer, take both breasts." I should have won an Oscar for that one.

My doctor said, "If I had more patients like you, I would have more women alive today."

Fortunately, that tumor, though gigantic, bigger than my breast alone, was benign. Unfortunately, I had tumors in both breasts and had to have some serious surgery and some reconstruction.

I was still recovering from that, and it hurt less to lie on my side. No one, especially me, thought to mention this before the current procedure, nor did I receive a complete physical exam. It turned out that lying in that position had caused blood to pool on one side of my head, which made it confusing for the doctors to see where the origin of this bleed was.

Consensus was that it might have been a small aneurysm that had bled out and clotted itself off. In fact, that was what

Dr. Jackass had told the press. The pain was still so wildly intense that I was put on a 24/7 drip of Dilaudid, which is a kind of synthetic heroin. I was in and out of consciousness. I don't know whether it was sleep or drugs or a coma, but I was hearing the song "Bridge Over Troubled Water" and falling through what looked like piles of colored fabric, and sometimes I saw pieces of the movie *Cinema Paradiso,* and sometimes I heard the voice of a woman I used to work with in Hollywood, a publicist named Pat Kingsley, who was talking to me in the kindest and most soothing way.

We were now on day five of my brain bleed and I had been coming and going. I had been "sleeping" more than waking. I had not eaten since the initial incident. Every time I woke up the television that hung from the ceiling blared with images of plane crashes and terror alerts—do you remember those colors? Many times I was unsure of what was real and what was my own nightmare. Suffering was all around me. I was still in the intensive-care wheel. Each of us there was fighting for life. Every person on all sides of me was crying out, moaning, whimpering, praying, and screaming.

After a couple more days, I was unable to get up, stand up, or think clearly and function. I had lost 18 percent of my body mass, according to the scale that my bed was on. Still, I guess some of the staff thought I was faking it. Being an actress and all—hey, I know; it comes with the territory. Some people imagine that because you can act in a film, you just act in your day-to-day life. Some people forget that when you're working, you are playing what is written by other people, and get several tries before someone says, "Print." By then, I was just too strung out and disoriented to try to explain this again. It was getting more and more difficult to see and to hear. But the general consensus was that I should go on home and stop faking it.

One of the nurses came in and bathed me and washed my hair. This act of kindness was so important to me, as everyone had stopped touching me, except my friend Stefanie Pleet, who would come and hold my hand and touch my face. For some reason she just knew that I needed to be touched. I think everyone else thought that I was too fragile.

This is where it gets weird, and I hesitate to share this with you, but I want you to believe in yourself and your instincts no matter how they come to you. So here goes.

One night I awoke to my grandmother Lela standing at the foot of my bed. I know that sounds reasonable, except my grandmother had been dead for thirty years. She looked beautiful. She smelled beautiful: she always wore Guerlain perfume, Shalimar. She was at her best, wearing her favorite suit and hat.

She said, "We don't really know what's wrong with you—we are working on it. But whatever you do, don't move your neck." Then she was gone.

I took the teddy bear my dad had brought me, squiggled to the side of the bed, and stuffed that bear by my neck and *DID NOT MOVE*. No matter what, I immobilized myself. I did *not* roll onto my side.

Mimi came to the hospital, because she thought I was being discharged. Until then, she had been running my household, keeping an eye on my son and the rest of my family. I whispered to her, "I'm dying! Get them to do something! I'm dying! Mimi, please help me!"

She looked at me and I could see that this was a big ask. She's shyer than I am, which is something, as when I am not busy being Sharon Stone, I am rather shy. But she knew I was serious and she knew that I meant it. She talked to everyone, my family and friends and the doctors. She says after she pulled "a full Shirley MacLaine" at the nurses' station, finally everyone agreed to another angiogram, in which once again a camera would be inserted into my femoral artery, this time on the other side. It would travel up the length of my body to get another look at my brain.

They said it would be a thirty-to-forty-five-minute procedure. For them it sounded like they had found a way to get this weird famous person out of the hospital and off their backs. Except when they went in, they found that my right vertebral artery, which is one of the two connecting your head to your back and spine, was torn to a fine shred and I was bleeding into my face, my brain, my head, and my spine. I had already had a significant stroke. And here we were at day nine of the bleed.

There was no opportunity to wake me for a consultation. It had gone far too far. My family had some hard decisions. They were faced with incomprehensible medical and ethical choices, and were told that any decision could potentially kill me on the spot. The artery could complete its rupture at any moment and I could die or it could rupture and clot off. They could put coils in place of the artery and possibly save my life or the process itself could kill me. All the while, the blood was rushing into my brain and my spine and my facial cavity at an ever-increasing rate. Either way, I had a 1 percent chance of survival.

They did such a great job. They stuck together, as they always do when it really matters. My father taught us a lesson early on. He said, "A family is like a hand: if one finger is cut, the whole hand bleeds." This has served us well. Nine hours later, I left the operating chamber without a vertebral artery and with twenty-three platinum coils in its place.

I woke up in my room knowing my grandmother had saved my life. She had put her hand on my family and on me and guided us through. My mother had held my hand and held my face like a lioness without ever entering the operating room; my sister had carried my heart and made hard, modern decisions on my behalf; and my father guarded every space and took care of everyone as only a father can do. Mimi went beyond her shyness and became her very best. The astonishing love and steadiness of my friends, solid as rocks, held me to this earth.

When I had been in the first emergency room and was bathed in the white light, I saw many people who had crossed over before. They told me what it would be like. I felt so safe, so immeasurably at peace, and yet I was pulled back into this life, this world. It was so confusing and harsh, and yet now I know that we are not far apart; they are not far away. We do not lose their love. We are love.

Those who I stayed with and for are my greatest lessons, teachers, and guides. And not only the easy ones. Those who I got to live for are a world full of love and light. You are my reason. Those who have come into my life since with similar stories, some in different phases of this story, light up my world. The love that I thought I didn't have, in fact I had. Just not as I had imagined it, not as the story has been told and retold a hundred million times to so many of us, making everything else we have done seem so small by comparison.

I found a love that was so much more: a real love, a true love. No, I didn't get the fairy tale. I got real life.

What Is Home

Kelly and I have a joke when folks ask us where we grew up. We say somewhere between Pithole and Tidioute, which is in fact true. But now I think it was really somewhere between naïveté and hopefulness. On a more literal level, where we were from was the first house across the city line into Meadville.

It was a tough town. We had bars and churches, a zipper factory, and the Erie-Lackawanna Railroad. After all, these were port towns, where hookers and heroin and everything bad got dropped off and no one looked back. Of course we had Allegheny College, the fancy school that no one who lived there could afford to go to. This was for out-of-towners. People more important than we were. I went to school in Saegertown, the next town over, the smaller town, the town with no stoplight. Both towns were in Amish country, with wagons, bonnets, and beards going by.

We got our milk from the dairy, our produce fresh from the acre-wide garden my mother planted by hand, and our protein from whatever my dad hunted. We ate deer all winter, rabbit and turkey and trout in spring and fall. When PETA complained that I wore fur, I was dumbstruck. As Karl Lagerfeld once said to me, "It's the original fabric, darling."

We lived in the "snowbelt," where the snow could drift up over our windows; then we would have to climb out a window to shovel the snow away from the doors to get out. The snow then turned to slush, which is a brown and wet mess of ice, dirt, snow, and misery. This was when the men wore galoshes over their shoes or boots, big, black rubber overboots with a zipper. Sexy. Then the slush turned to ice, and just before spring it became black ice, which is the most dangerous road hazard. This was when a lot of people died in car and especially motor-cycle accidents. It still is.

Spring was always a great relief. I like spring in Pennsylva-nia, I like tulips and daffodils, I like nature. As a child, I loved running up and down the big ravine next to our house. The creek below was the great divide—the dividing line between the cities. So, while it wasn't big, it was *big*.

It was huge to me, Mike, Pat, and Kelly. When Kelly was a teenager, she used to climb out of the window and jump off the roof to go to parties. My sister is quite a character—she was when she was a little girl and she is now. If there is a party, Kelly is either at it or giving it. If Kelly had a mob name it would be Kelly Party. She thinks up the most elaborate ideas for parties: it is not unusual for Kelly to have synchronized swimmers in her swimming pool or a party where everyone invited could come dressed in East Indian clothing and try the cuisine of that culture or another. She too dreams of seeing the world. Kelly wears feather boas like most of us wear watches.

I feel lucky to have Mike. I always think that cool girls have a big brother. That's how you learn to hang with the guys. I grew up hangin' with the guys. They couldn't get rid of me. Still can't. They get to do all the good stuff. Who wants to shop when you can do sports and drive too fast and eat a lot and sleep on the couch while golf is on?

Mike had a newspaper route, and I thought that was so cool and I always wanted to go with him. One wonderful morning, he invited me. We got up very early and Mike had sewn me my own paper-route bag. It held exactly one copy of *The Meadville Tribune,* or as it was called in those days, the *Tribune-Republican.* We had breakfast at the kitchen table. There was a giant lilac tree outside the window, and while we were eating our cereal, a big blue jay flew into the window. I so vividly remember the blue of the jay and the purple of the lilacs and my one paper pressed against my breast, my heart thumping with adrenaline.

Later, when Mike got in trouble and the world seemed so confused and both he and I felt so lost, that memory pulled me through. I was sure that Mike, the one who sewed a paper bag for a five-year-old girl, was a very good person, and I held on. Now that we are much older and I know that all of who I am is wrapped up in growing up with him there—looking after me, nosing me into the hipper choices, helping me make friends when I wasn't good at it, standing up for me, protecting me—I see that blue jay for all he was.

Patrick is my little brother. I remember not long after he was born: it was so exciting. We were playing with a yellow toy truck. I put him in the bed of it. I was pulling him, then I was pushing him; he barely fit in the small plastic space in the back of the truck. We were going so fast; the air was touching his body and making him feel good, making him laugh. I didn't know I was doing anything bad. He was kind of squished up and his diaper was on a little bit sideways, but I kept running and pulling the handle, singing a song I thought he might like; I was watching over him, making sure he was having a good time. I was happy to have a baby brother. I was seven.

Then the yellow plastic slats on the right side of the truck broke. It seemed like they broke in slow motion, splintering away as he tumbled the enormous, cliff-like six inches down to the carpeted floor below. I raced like, well . . . I wanted to race like Jesse Owens, but in my fear and panic I raced more like Jackie Mason. Trying to catch him and think of my alibi all at the same time. He fell on the floor like a dumpling. He didn't even cry. I thought he was dead.

I stood there so terrified and hurt, convinced I was a seven-year-old baby killer. I am scarred to this day. My mom ran into the room. "Jesus Christ, I can't leave you alone for a goddamn minute, what the hell are you doing?"

Good question: What the hell was I doing? Was anyone going to tell me if the dumpling was alive? Or was the persecution going to take priority here? She picked him up; he made a baby sound, and I almost puked.

As my kid brother started to grow, he got pretty darn big and real handsome: the big, handsome, quiet type. The type who all of the girls like and all of the guys are a little intimidated by because they don't quite understand why he's bigger than they are and why all of the girls like this quiet guy. He was smart and really funny—and he wrote his letters backward.

In those days it took a long time for anyone to figure out that this was called dyslexia, something that happens to a few special smart kids. Now they would call it a learning disorder. At that time everyone just got mad, confused, and scared. And they abused my brother. His backward letter writing caused him quite a bit of trouble with reading and with teachers who weren't kind. They tormented him, made him stand in front of the room wearing a dunce cap. Assholes. It's quite astonishing, really, to observe how much people enjoy themselves at a child's expense. I guess that is the unimaginable depth of insecurity. The whole experience made him shy.

I just knew that it was because I had dropped him out of the side of the yellow truck. It was my fault and I knew it, and nothing at all would ever change the fact that I had made my brother write his letters backward. I was so ashamed. No doctor telling me that bouncing a kid six inches onto a carpet wasn't the cause of the problem could make me feel any better. No statistics did the trick; deep down I knew there had to be a reason, because he seemed perfect in every other way. Patrick is the best of all four of us kids. He is the kindest, the most generous, the softest of heart, the best to our folks. And my best friend.

When we were kids, my dad built us all a tree house in the old oak tree. We climbed up wooden slats to get to the bunk beds. They were made on pipes that we put army canvas on. We pulled them out to sleep and put them back on their closed slats when we hung out in there to play dolls or cards. There was a back door with a rope with a lot of big knots for our hands and feet, so we could swing out of the tree house and across the ravine, jumping all the way to the other side of the creek. And, in fact, to the other town, Meadville.

After several years the tree was hit by lightning. My dad was standing under it at the time and the lightning got him too. Then a few years later, it came for me. I was ironing my uniform for my waitressing job at the Big Boy restaurant. I had one hand on the spigot and the other holding the iron, filling it with the water that came straight from our well when lightning hit the well. It threw me across the kitchen and into the fridge. My mother screamed and slapped me across the face.

I kind of passed out and came to at the same time. She had restarted my heart. I still have a skip in the beat.

But when lightning struck the tree-house tree, we simply hoisted the little house down and it became Kelly's and my playhouse. Dad laid in a concrete walkway for us and Mom put flower planters in the windows and drapes made from old kitchen towels.

In summer I put on plays in the driveway. This is when the director in me was born. Each garage stall was a set. The picnic table became the seats: one bench in front and one on top of the table, creating three haphazard rows. My poor, tormented sister was often the harried star of these home-written plays, as were her friends and all the neighbor kids.

I used parts of songs on my old 45 record player for dramatic effect. For stage lighting, I commandeered the work lights, hanging from the garage rafters, that we used when we took cars apart. Costumes could be made from kitchen toweling or bath mats, swimsuits, fur hats, anything that I wouldn't later catch a beating for taking. These hats and objects could be found hanging from any of the many mounted animal heads all over our house. These deceased, dusty animals would get lighted noses and various decorations throughout the year.

There is still something about the sound of a screen door banging. I can taste summer and long nights out running around capturing lightning bugs in mason jars.

In my family, we all had seasonal jobs and responsibilities. One of mine was to repaint the barn. Painting it was nothing. Stripping that old barn of the old paint—now, that was something.

I also had to mow the lawn. At age ten, I got on the John Deere riding lawn mower, threw it into gear, dropped the blade, and made beautiful patterns in the lawn as I mowed our two acres. I kind of enjoyed it; it felt like a privilege to make the property pretty, the grass perfect. We had a U-shaped driveway. That long two-tire-track drive came down in and around the house, between the garage, which was in front of the barn, and the back of the house. My mother planted peony bushes on both sides, and it was gorgeous. There was a huge weeping willow on the side of the house and that massive old oak in the far yard.

When autumn came, the trees in the ravine turned and it was so beautiful, alive with color. When you grow up in the East, autumn is just enchanting: everything looks like it's on fire. We raked huge piles of leaves on the front lawn and jumped in them. We just raked and jumped in the brisk fall air. I loved that. Apple cider days, almost time to go to the creek (or the "crick," as we called it) for ice for our homemade ice cream.

Another one of my usual jobs was to carry the trash down to the burning barrels behind the barn and sort it. This way the non-burnables could go to the dump. We had to do this ourselves. I liked this job best in fall. When it was a little bit cold, I could throw all of the glass through the flames and smash it in the big, rusty metal barrels. It felt so cathartic. I would throw and scream.

But when winter came, and I had to haul anything through the snow, I hated it. We had to walk across the property in the morning to get the bus. We were soaked before we even got on, wet half of the day at school. It was dark on the bus coming home at day's end. Ours was a school where kids drove in on their tractors after completing their chores. Our school, all eighty-seven of us. Yippee. I felt like an oddball.

How odd, you may wonder? Well, when we all had to learn a poem and most of the kids came proudly with *I think that I shall never see / A poem lovely as a tree,* I solemnly recited every stanza of "Annabel Lee," to my teacher's horror—especially as I went on and on relentlessly. This was only topped by next year's show-and-tell. I found a bat trapped on our porch and caught it with a dustpan and broom and put it, live, into a big mason jar with some bits of grass. Proudly I banged some holes in the top with a screwdriver so it could breathe, then secreted it to school and hid it in my desk, waiting for my big reveal.

This too was met with horror: the kids screamed, the teacher panicked. "You can't have that here!!!"

I skulked to my desk and shoved it back inside.

At recess I figured I had better get rid of it. Not realizing at my tender age that bats were nocturnal, I released it on the playground. The poor bat flying without his radar was buzzing all of the kids, hitting them in the head, chaos ensuing. . . .

Yes, I was odd, but not on purpose. A feeling that I have come to realize had nothing to do with my environment. Nor, I now realize, was I the only one.

When I was five I was placed in the second grade, which was not a decision met with a big hallelujah from anyone. There was no thrill from the administration saying, "Wow, we have an exceptional child," just the knowing nods from the members of the school board, who made the decision for me, and the principal, who hated it but did it anyway. My parents were frightened; I was, well, different. This experiment did not go well or happily for anybody. After a few less-than-extraordinary months, all agreed I should go to first grade like every other little kid (though they were still older than I was) and learn how to go to school. So all of my belongings were stuffed into my desk/chair combo, and I was put in the chair and slid down the hall to the first grade. Efficient, I suppose, but humiliating, I have to say.

Moving to first grade didn't go well either. I got in trouble for being ahead of the rest of the class. In trouble again for teaching another girl named Sharon how to write cursive. You can see how that turned out, obviously, as this is now becoming a secret analog language of the past.

I was in trouble all the time for doing that wholly unfeminine thing of *thinking*. I was just thinking left and right, and if that wasn't enough, I was telling people about it—and there is nothing more annoying than a five-year-old ex–second grader telling you that she read about it elsewhere. Yes, I was the kid they make fun of in movies. That one. The little annoying know-it-all. The one who doesn't know that she is so goddamn irritating.

So I became the school's personal science project. Every new invention was tried on me. The "speed-reading machine" was one of the first tryouts. It was not much of a machine: I had to turn the crank on the side for the pages to go by "super-fast."

Little did they know that my mom was already way ahead on this one: she'd been trying to train up my psychic ability since I was about two, and I could do almost the whole deck of cards by the time they got to me.

Hey, if I could get out of the dishes by getting the numbers right, I was getting it. I could do numbers forward, backward, inside out. It was just a card trick, after all.

I grew up not knowing my mother. In fact, I grew up not liking my mother. She was efficient and taught me how to do everything: to cook, to clean, to sew, to bake, to plant and garden, to can food, to put away the clothes in perfect order, to make beds, to do laundry, to set the table, to serve the meal, to put on my makeup, to set my hair, to be ready at all times, to do what I was told when I was told to do it and right then, not ten minutes later. She watched me do it to make sure it was done correctly, and if it wasn't, I did it again. If I sassed her, she slapped me into the next week. If I moved when getting my hair combed or brushed out, the brush could be and was broken over my head.

I grew to hate her. Not only for that but for her coldness.

I knew she had grown up with a different family than her siblings had, having been given to another family when she was nine years old. I thought it was because they were so poor. What I didn't know, until now, until I wrote this book and needed to try to talk to her, was her truth. The truth she was too ashamed to tell anyone. The truth, I'm sure, she had never told her own husband, my dad.

Her father had begun to beat her when she was five years old. She wanted to go to a ball game with her sisters. She asked her mother, who said, Ask your father, who said, Ask your mother, who had already left for the day to work as a housekeeper. So she went with her sisters, and when she got home, her father took her out in the yard and struck her first with a belt and then with berry-bush branches. Even the leaves have thorns.

My mother at six would have been the type of thin only rickets and scurvy can create. Imagine a young girl during the Depression, coming from a house so close to the railroad tracks that the passengers could reach into the two-bedroom home that slept her, her parents, and her three siblings. Well, two siblings, after a drunk driver hit my mother's younger sister so hard that he knocked her right out of my mother's hand, and when her sister landed she was dead.

My mother? She came home to tell the news. She already had a reputation as the bearer of bad tidings, having been an in-utero twin of the birth sign Gemini whose sister was stillborn.

I picture her standing in the kitchen, carrying news no full-weighted man could bear, chilled by the icebox kept cold with the ice blocks only sometimes delivered, telling her beaten-down mother her daughter was dead. The drunk driver? He showed up drunk again the next day, having slept in his clothes, to say how sorry he was, wilted flowers clutched in his hand. My grandmother promptly walked outside and threw them in the outhouse.

My maternal grandfather, Clarence, said nothing, nothing at all. After all, who would bury this child? Not the welfare office, where my grandmother walked with her young children miles from home each day to feed them. Not the school, which didn't care if they became anything at all. Not the neighbors; my grandfather had already produced far more children than they would prefer, both with and without them.

Clarence continued to beat my mother. By the time she was seven and had to sing "Jesus Loves Me" alone at church, she was unable to do so without crying all the way through and got a standing ovation. No one knew why they were standing. Had God pulled them to their feet?

When she was nine, as she was taking off her green one-piece gym suit in the changing room at school, one of the other girls saw her back, so badly torn and scarred, and told the gym teacher. She came and lifted my mom's shirt and promptly took her to the principal's office. My mom was asked what happened. She told them that her father beat her often in the yard with berry-bush branches. That he liked to take them outside for beatings so that the neighbors could see. Years later, crying as she confessed this to me, she said, "My mother tried to pro-tect me from . . . I don't know which is worse, being molested or being beaten, 'cause they're both kind of the same."

Social services, even in hillbilly country, moved my mother out. They put her with a family where the wife and mother had asthma and couldn't fulfill her own duties. My mom became their live-in cook, laundress, grocery shopper—all at age nine. She got up before school and hung the clothes on the line and walked the two to three miles to school and walked home after to do the ironing and make dinner before she could start her homework.

The husband, a dentist, offered to fix her teeth, which were rotting from malnutrition, and she said that she would hand-wash and starch his dental jackets and do his accounting in return. This was when she was twelve. He said she didn't have to, but her mother had told her that nothing is for free.

She tells me about how much they did for her, how she always called them "Mr." and "Mrs." for the whole time she lived there, until she married my father at sixteen and moved out. She says they had food, they lived respectfully. Mom tells me that they saved her, that she would have killed herself if they hadn't taken her in. And that no one will ever hit her again.

She reminds me that before, living with her own parents, she only ever got an orange for Christmas. The shame of poverty, of abuse, of being unloved made her feel so undeserving.

Three generations of Irish-American maids, immigrants who felt so undeserving that they lived in this horrible way. I didn't understand what my mother was doing when she taught me her trade, her skills, when she told me that I would have to stand on my "own two goddamn feet," that no one would be there to take care of me. I didn't know that this was how she knew how to love, and that this was the best love she had ever gotten.

My mother, a raven-haired, ivory-skinned, blue-eyed beauty, taken for everything. Giving so much for so little in return.

My mother, who wrote me thank-you notes all of my adult life that hurt my feelings because I just wanted her to love me. I didn't understand the notes. The gratitude. It didn't make sense: Why wouldn't I give her everything I could? Why wouldn't I spoil my mom? I didn't want a thank-you note, I wanted a hug, I wanted her affection. But who had ever given any affection to her? Clearly no one.

The dentist's wife gave her one of her suits to wear to the movies, and my mother talks to me about this with such nostalgia, as if this was the moment of greatest love for her. And I believe that it was. Now I get it. It kills me, and I get it.

I understand her quiet nature, her sense of removal—what I used to see as coldness—why she talks to my housekeepers more than she does to me. But until now, God, until now, I only thought, *She just doesn't like me or love me.*

My mother grew up in poverty, the kind of hillbilly, Depression-era poverty that made America into the greedy America it is today. The kind of heartbreaking poverty that frightened a nation, a world, into madness, darkness, and the kind of depravity that exists right now.

Her father worked pouring hot metal in a big, open factory.

As a little girl, I would walk through the parking lot and see the men in their asbestos suits and those helmets with flaps down over the shoulders and glass in front of the eyes, reflecting only the red; the long, fireproof gloves for lifting the huge pots of fiery ore: now a liquid that made me feel like I was looking into hell. I could feel the heat in the parking lot. Hear that oppressive sound of clanking metal and pounding machines.

My father, on the other hand, came from a super-rich family: oil drillers. Some of the first: from Oil City, Pennsylvania, there right at the start. They were gorgeous. My grandmother Lela wore Schiaparelli clothing, silk hose, beautiful shoes; she carried handbags, not purses. She had beautiful dove-gray gloves that I admired terribly, which she took off and placed over her handbag perfectly. She wore real jewelry, and that Shalimar perfume that she sprayed in the air and walked through.

Her husband, Joseph Stone II, was in the oil business with his brother, John. They were wildcat drillers, successful and handsome, elegant. The photos of them are in oval gilded frames, and in them they sit as children on gilded chairs in hosiery and knee-length pants, suit coats with the traditional flower placed on the lapel. Of the women in the family, only my grandmother had her portrait done with this type of style and sophistication. In my great-grandmother's photograph, she is standing on a hillside, elderly and worn, as though she had created the hills themselves.

While my grandfather and great-uncle were out drilling wells, my grandmother Lela was running the business. While not typically beautiful, Lela was handsome and strong-willed, her humor tough and contagious. She ran her hillside as her mother had done before her when the family first arrived.

Then all of the family's riches were lost in one terrible explosion, one miscalculation. My grandfather died and Lela lost everything because, as a woman, she couldn't inherit. Instead, the family business was given to my great-uncle's son, an eighteen-year-old kid. In two years, it was all gone. The business. My grandmother's home, the family estate her mother had earned with the money she brought from Ireland, all of it.

Lela was brilliant, but because women didn't count, all of her hard work building one of the first oil-drilling businesses ever seen in Oil City, Pennsylvania, was simply swept aside, and all of her knowledge and labor with her husband destroyed by the fact of her gender. She had three small children and she had to go to work in an asylum. The eldest, my aunt Vonne, went with her; at the time she was seven or eight. My dad, who was four or five, went with his younger brother to live with their grandma and her dog, and then, after she died, to live in people's barns, in their horse stalls, so they could work for food and blankets.

Yet there was no taking the lady out of my grandmother. And there was no taking the gentleman out of my father. His aristocratic temperament was part of his profile, part of his beauty and style, as much as my mother's raw wildness was the driving force of hers. Though he didn't live the privileged life past four years of age, it was never not part of him: his to regain, his to be known for and by, his to understand what it was and why it was gone.

Joe Stone quite literally laid my foundation. Then there are the codings of his siblings, his mother, and all the rest of them. I am primarily Irish with a good pound of Scandinavian, and, so I've recently read, 8 percent French. I often wonder which bits of me grew from which parts as I travel around the world and see those places and meet those folks. It's surprising how similar we all are once we scratch the surface.

Which reminds me of an old Irish toast my friend Brooklyn told me: "I'm more of who I am now than I was when I got here."

I think as I get older, I'm getting closer to the center of my onion, the soul of my heart.

Style

When I was in my twenties, my boyfriend's best friend told me his simple theory of relationships: men are stupid and women are crazy. Full of the arrogance of youth and the power of beauty, I did not stop to consider myself in this equation. Though he and I remained friends to the day he died.

Many years have passed, and although I do not ascribe to the "crazy" theory, I do easily accept that I could be seen as a quirky broad. And men? Well, since my quirkiness is in large part a result of my interaction with this tribe, I leave that judgment to them.

I think back to my first big sexual encounter with the opposite sex. I was in the first grade. I was on my way out to recess and a little boy hid behind the staircase and leapt out and grabbed me and kissed me. I was shocked, and scared. He ran out to the playground, leaving me alone in the dank and dark stairwell. I stood there stunned and confused. Suddenly I was overcome with rage. I began to walk slowly out to the playground, hearing the sounds of the other children playing. I saw him. I stalked up to him. He was frozen. I grabbed his arm and bit him as hard as I could and walked away.

I was sent home from school and given several days off to consider my actions. Everyone thought I was crazy. He never said what he had done. I never told on him. No one ever asked me.

When I was a kid we all thought Nubby Neuwirth was an idiot. Not an idiot savant, as we now celebrate. This was back when he used to talk to his lunch box at the bus stop. In fact, we used to hit him with it. The lunch box, not the bus stop, in case you're an idiot too.

We would walk through wet snow in the frigid dark and wait for that cigarette-smoking lady driver to open the bus door. A charming good morning to you children.

At least May Kent got on four stops later. We always sat together and everybody knew it. May was a classic "mean girl," and for a while I felt lucky to be friends with her, because that meant she wouldn't be mean to me. Once May filled marshmallows with cayenne pepper and gave them to the girl who always tried to sit with us. That was the end of her compulsion to befriend us.

After that, Pixie Fallon moved to our town, which was good because I was sick of May being mean and, anyway, she was going to marry her cousin David. Pixie just appeared. Her family had moved into a big house down the dirt road that the bus drove on, and one day she just got on. Instantly noticeable, with that strange white hair. And those pie eyes: blue, like teacups, and white skin and freckles. Yet you could tell she was no Goody Two-Shoes. I looked at her and it was on.

Pixie was my first real friend. We did everything together. We ran away from boys, rode horses, and ran around nude in the woods with scarves tied around our necks. I don't know why.

We stayed overnight with each other. We taught each other's little brothers to French-kiss. In the middle of the night, her father would invariably run through the living room, where we were all sleeping on the floor. He was usually attired in only a pair of tattered Fruit of the Looms, which added just the perfect touch to his particular form of paternal insanity.

You see, Pixie's family were Jehovah's Witnesses and basically she wasn't allowed to do anything. Her father was convinced that boys were sneaking around in the backyard trying to see us. We so hoped it was true. It wasn't. Later we realized that his actions were propelled by his own faithlessness and deceit. He eventually had a baby with my uncle Gene's best friend's wife. My uncle's best friend then tried to shoot Pixie's dad and went to jail. Small towns.

My uncle died many years later—actually, the day before *Basic Instinct* premiered. He wasn't really murdered, like people thought. It was just the bloody trail in the snow and the way he was lying there, frozen, the truck door open, blood smeared down the side of the seat. There was something about the way he seemed to be sleeping there on the front steps of his cottage that made it seem that much more gruesome, that much more lonely and wrong. His jacket falling open, his plaid shirt half-unbuttoned, his hair falling gently onto his forehead simply seemed to say, *Hey I just tripped,* but the twenty-foot slide of blood coming off his rubber galoshes seemed to disagree.

It wasn't the first time my uncle's behavior was awkward for us. There was the time he put a gun to his head and called up and said he was going to kill himself. We had to go over and talk to him while he just sat there in his baggy underwear and an old shirt, with that gun to his head, talking about his wife for what seemed like hours. This killing-oneself business is a very time-consuming situation, and, I have found, somewhat boring after the initial *Jesus, what are you doing?* crisis moment passes. I guess that's why my mom says, "People who threaten to kill themselves . . . should." I never know if I should laugh when she says that. If you knew my family you would understand. Maybe after reading this book, you will.

Gene was a wonderful guy, really, even though it doesn't sound like it right now. He was the funny one, the joker, the tickler, the ice-cream buyer. He had a great car, a convertible; oh, how we loved that car. If we got lucky, we could go out to Hank's and get a sherbet cone; I was just mad about orange sherbet. I thought orange sherbet was so exotic and sophisticated, and I would get one and we could ride home with the top down and sometimes (I'm guessing when he was a bit drunk) he would stand up while he drove. I thought that was quite sophisticated too.

He had joined the navy at fifteen, after the oil well blew and all, and had fantastic tattoos to show for it. There was one in particular that I thought was very provocative: a naked girl in a martini glass that ran the whole length of his right shin. That was a wow. He had the word SWEET over one nipple and SOUR over the other; that made summer just a hoot for me. Of course there was a dirty word on his knuckles.

Now, in retrospect, we might not have known such a fantastic guy with tattoos and all who drove standing up if he hadn't been my dad's brother. But he was. And you know, family is family, and when my family got together, it was thick. They settled into the kitchen and told stories. Mike used to hunch down at the top of the stairs and try to learn the jokes so he could tell them at school on Monday. I never thought Mike was that funny, but then again, he's the one who held me down and spit on me.

Gene was my dad's little brother, but no one ever called him Gene. We all called him "Uncle Beaner." Just because he ate a lot of beans in the navy, everybody said. I think that is an awful name, but that was his moniker: Beaner. Good old Uncle Beaner. Frozen to the concrete steps of his little white cottage surrounded by yellow tape, and no one could move him for about twenty-four hours because it was considered a crime scene.

So the family was just standing around in parkas trying to be helpful and somehow normal and comprehend Uncle Beaner lying over there in a ball with the truck door open, and no one could close the door or pick him up or hug him or fix it or change a thing.

It wasn't murder, but in a way it was a crime. The horrible crime of loneliness. You see, Uncle Beaner's wife, Dorothy, had died a very slow and tortured death from cancer, back in the days when people didn't say "cancer" out loud. Ladies just whispered, "the C-word," and my aunt shrank and shrank and eventually died at sixty pounds of pain. They gave me her clothes to wear to high school. They stank of cigarettes, and that doesn't come out.

Uncle Beaner was simply meant to go on. Except he didn't know how. So he drove standing up and put a gun to his temple sometimes. And went to a bar and got drunk and fell getting into his truck and hit his head and drove home and got out of his truck and fell again and hit his head and fell down on the front steps of his little white cottage and froze to death.

The only person who ever called Uncle Beaner his real name, Gene, was his older sister, my aunt Vonne. My father's whole family was extremely good-looking: dark hair, light eyes, and those faces. Lela made good-looking children, and they were all fireballs: smart, quick-witted, and athletic. All three of them were hilarious, and they loved to make my grandmother laugh. But they were tight knit and didn't let people in easily.

Vonne was exceptionally beautiful; I thought she looked like a Spanish dancer, with her long black hair and red lips. She loved to ski and took us skiing and golfing. She taught us the skills of refined wealth. This could explain why I gravitated toward marrying a professional skier who had become a producer, who was good-looking, smart, quick-witted, with dark hair and green eyes. My first husband looked like and acted like those family trips. The supposed ideal.

Vonne was also a scholar and a talented painter. She painted murals around my grandmother's big and rangy home. She had tons of fabulous, interesting books and paints and brushes and canvases and energy to give to me. She lived on the other side of a small and scary wood next to my grandmother's. To get to her house, I had to run through those woods for about five or six minutes, during which time it got darker and then just dark before I could see the safety of the approaching house. It was like some kind of courage-building ritual; if you wanted to be in the group, you had to be cool enough to make it through the woods. I sucked it up and ran like a maniac, or sometimes I just walked and tried to see if I could figure out the whole tree-by-tree thing of it all and conquer my fears. Neither worked: the trees were gigantic, the forest was dense, the path was small, no sunlight was getting in there. The test was the test of being with myself; it was fantastic to run at least once, if not several times, daily and then to arrive on the doorstep of either of these extraordinary dames.

My aunt had built a rather modern house on her end of the wood. Large and contemporary, for herself and her husband—an Italian man—and their daughter. She had been quite the catch: one failed suitor had landed in Grandma's backyard in a helicopter just to try to take Aunt Vonne on a date. Everyone was wondering who would finally be the one to domesticate my wild and feline aunt; I don't think anyone thought it would be this short, somewhat rotund Italian guy. But he was a terrific man, and he won her hook, line, and sinker, as they say where I am from. When he died she looked at me with tears in her eyes and said, "You know, I never remembered to cheat on George?" We laughed with so much tenderness and so much deep love for him. She had loved him so profoundly and he had captured her so completely.

I am named for her—my middle name is Vonne—and in many ways she was like a mother to me. She was always brutally honest about herself, her faults, her strengths, and her beliefs. I believe she was a better woman and a deeper soul than she ever came to really be known for. There is such a prejudice against real beauty, especially when it comes with real intelligence, like it did with my aunt. She was always coming from behind that. She made a lot of jokes at her own expense. Meanwhile she had two master's degrees, won beauty pageants, and successfully ran her own two businesses. She also survived two radical mastectomies and went right back to skiing.

Of course she was her mother's daughter. My grandmother Lela was really something. Although she was just over five feet tall, she was a force to be reckoned with. I thought she just hung the moon. I wanted to spend every minute with her. I started to live with her every summer when I was a very little girl of about four or five. She and Aunt Vonne would just take me. I don't even remember packing; I know my mother never packed my clothes. I just remember the excitement in the car, like a getaway car, driving a little fast with the radio on, quiet at first and then the laughter; we'd done it again. Sometimes they would come when my mom wasn't home; then my heart would race: it was like the day was brighter than normal and a little bit faster, the sounds crisper. I could hear the car coming from far away, the breeze in the trees. It was wonderful. I felt so wanted, so incredibly loved.

Lela would sit quite regally in the kitchen, waiting; I guess Aunt Vonne was upstairs packing my things. I seem to remember that I was floating out of my body, around the green apple tree and down by the stream in the ravine next to the house, picking daffodils from the embankment to leave in a vase in the kitchen window without a note. This was my secret sign to my mother that I had gone with them, a way to let her know not to worry.

Then we were gone, leaving my two brothers and little sister behind. I was someone's favorite. I mattered somewhere; there were people who thought that the way I thought and talked and did things was interesting and valuable. They liked me. It was so extraordinary to live in their world.

My grandmother had a gang of kooks for friends. There was a very tall woman with gray hair and light gray cat-eyed glasses on a tiny colored-stone chain and gray dresses and gray bags whom my grandmother loved to death but about whom she would say, "She is so nosy she would smell our farts to see what we had for lunch." She had another lady friend who wore shoes with turned-up toes with bells on them and about twenty necklaces and colored silk pants and as many as three silky colorful shirts at a time. I used to sit under the table and watch their shoes and listen to them too.

I have such vivid memories of taking up residence under the tree next to Lela's south porch. It was an enormous blue spruce. That tree was probably forty feet tall and twelve to fifteen feet in diameter, and the low branches hung to the ground. I would crawl in under the branches with my books and pillow and blanket, and there I would spend my afternoon.

"Knock knock knock," Grandma would say. "I have a special delivery."

I would laugh uproariously. "Okay, what is it?"

And in she would push a tiny (stolen—hang on, you'll see) bowl full of maraschino cherries covered in whipped cream. Well, that was just the Cracker Jack best! I was tipsy with enthusiasm. "Please come in, Grandma," I would say, and in she would climb in her full Schiaparelli suit, complete with silk hose, skirt, and jacket, and sit under the tree with me, eating cherries. This was the greatest thing in the world. Her white hair was so beautiful. There has never before or since been a lady so beautiful as my grandmother. And certainly none so funny or devilish.

She taught me how to pickpocket and how to steal the things off a tabletop. Oh, I could put the entire dinner service in your bag while talking to you. Yes, I probably could pick a pocket with a bit of practice. Old light fingers. My grandmother was quite a character. Her kitchen had hotel china from all over the place, even the giant two-sided dinner-napkin holder. Huge salt and pepper shakers, monogrammed silverware from hotels. I bought silverware recently that said SPOON on the spoons, and so forth, just because it reminded me of her so much.

As I grew, she had odd jobs for me. She would have me take all of the dishes and glassware out so we could paint the inside of the cupboards. I was allowed to keep any change I might find inside. As I took out the glasses ever so carefully, I was amazed to find coins randomly in many of the various cups and glasses and all around on the plates and even way in the back. It was such a fantastic thing: the more I worked, the more and more change there was in there! She was very clever. She sat in the kitchen and talked to me the whole time, equally delighted with my discoveries, each new coin or glass of coins as thrilling and funny to her as to me and leading us to new and more amusing conversation.

One summer I was to take off all the storm windows and scrape and paint them. Of course I put my arm through one and cut myself. I had to replace the window. This was not a household for sissies. "Pay attention" was the lesson of the day. We were women who might well have to learn to take care of ourselves.

In spite of my uncle Beaner's friend's attempt to kill Pixie's father, I stayed close with her throughout my adolescence. She and Linda Whistler and Danny Weaver were my best friends. I needed only three.

Linda was super-brainy, and I loved to hang with her one-on-one. She liked to read and knew about everything, it seemed to me. We decided to set up a hot dog stand on the sidewalk at various baseball games in town. Or at least this was our front. Actually, we were campaigning for Democrats, passing out buttons, keeping a sign on the folding table that held our steam roaster for the hot dogs. We were in heaven.

My parents, especially my mother, thought it was odd that I would hang with only one friend for hours on end, and just talk. My sister jumping off the roof to go out with one of her best friends, Lorna, and their troop of pals was, in my mother's opinion, far more normal. My mother would show me the list of my sister's friends next to the kitchen phone and say, "Why can't you be more like your sister?" I don't think she considered grocery shopping with Danny a friendly outing.

Danny and I certainly did. Danny was my first gay friend.

We loved to shop together, and both of our mothers were often incapacitated for one reason or another. We would go to the supermarket and shop and dance. As our parents liked to watch *The Lawrence Welk Show,* we were quite familiar with Bobby and Cissy, who were not at all like Fred and Ginger. Nope, Bobby and Cissy were like dancing-mannequin porn. And Danny and I thought they were hilarious, and we could do all of their numbers. And do them we did: at the market to the Muzak.

We did so many good things together. We skipped school and went to Pittsburgh, where we rode the escalator. Repeatedly. I don't know if you can wholly appreciate what a hick-town beauty-queen-to-be I was that I enjoyed going up and down the escalator over and over and over and over and over yet again, but I can say that I recall it with so much enthusiasm.

Danny went on to produce *The Phil Donahue Show,* and to create the psychological aftercare for those who went on that show. He won awards for his breakthrough work. He was a deacon at his church and was in the same relationship for more than thirty years before he died of a neurological injury in 2018. It crushes me to say so. He struggled at the end. He was a good man. A great man. I loved him very much.

That love is a comfort to me. I know that the balm it now offers as I feel the wound of his loss will stay with me and transform this grief into something else.

As a middle child, I never got the new stuff, the one thing that everyone else had and I so desperately wanted. I just stood there and waited. I not only got hand-me-downs, I got hand-me-ups. But I had smarts and I had style.

Style is what you do with what's wrong with you. Barbra Streisand's nose, Clark Gable's ears, Danny DeVito's size, Cher. And let's face it, they are all loaded with style. Clear, crisp, finger-snappin' style washed to squeaky-clean perfection by years of heartache.

Those tears begin when you're a kid and you don't get what you then think of as the good thing and you quietly, courageously figure out how to make the thing you've got so fabulous that it becomes *the* thing, what everybody else just has to have. Except now, you've got the only one. Some of us have gone a long way on that ticket. Now it *is* the ticket; how the world has changed, thank God.

I was not one of the popular kids growing up. I was not part of that magical inner circle. But I remember observing those girls—and always, among them, *the* girl.

I have a very clear memory of the girl approaching me when we were in fifth grade. As she walked toward me I was filled with hope. A terrible kind of wanting. Her wavy hair was dusted with sunlight; she was smiling that kind of smile that seems to float and beckon like a siren from the shore. Her friends surrounded her like a Greek choir, singing and laughing, and all the while it seemed as if none of their feet were touching the ground at all.

My feet, per usual, felt as if they were made of concrete, or even more as if they were embedded in the concrete of the playground. My head was big, very, very big, so large and bulbous and big. I was alone, with my one other alone-friend and our books. We stared at them in wonder as they moved toward us. What could they possibly be doing?

They came closer and their laughter rang out: an American dream of happiness and belonging. My heart began to race, though my mind was stuck in a stupor of bewilderment and awe. The closer they came, the more fantastic the whole thing seemed.

Here they were, the loved ones. The pretty and the popular, the liked and the happy. The girls who had life figured out. The girls with the good shoes. The girls whose feet never hurt, the girls who boys always wanted, the girls who had friends who did and didn't like them and no one cared. The goddesses.

They were looking directly at me; *she* was looking directly at me, and smiling. Smiling at me, with that soft, happy, easy, inviting smile. I was trapped like a rabbit in a cage; I smiled back. She laughed her easy laugh and slowed down and ever so gently walked right up to me.

I was stunned in my gratitude that the goddesses were going to be my friends; they were going to include me. I started to open my mouth to speak, to say hello, and then, just then, she slapped me as hard as she possibly could across my face.

All of the junior goddesses laughed. They laughed so hard when they saw her handprint appear on my cheek. As all of her finger marks and thumbprint rose on my face, they laughed; as the tears welled in my astonished eyes, they laughed; as she turned and threw her shiny hair over her shoulder, they laughed. They laughed as she walked away.

As I sat with my back against the school wall waiting for the bell to end recess, I could hear them laughing and talking, and as I went to the girls' room to see my face in the mirror and to try to wash it off, I could hear them laughing and talking. For the rest of the day, I heard them laughing and talking.

When I became famous, *People* magazine did an interview and spoke to people in my town. She told them that when I was in school I was a snob.

The first time I went to the Cannes Film Festival, it was for *Total Recall.* My luggage never arrived. So I wore the pair of black wide-leg linen pants, black T-shirt, black cotton pullover, the huge, brightly painted silk scarf designed by my longtime secret boyfriend, and my black open-back, kitten-heel mules that I had worn on the plane in Oh So Many Different Ways for Oh So Many Different Days.

I should add that not one of the beautiful women present thought to offer me a hand here and lend me something of theirs.

I wasn't famous or important, but I was young and pretty and threatening. Apparently they thought the compliments I got from their fellows on my ingenuity were amusing enough for all of us to get by on. Even Robert Downey Jr. mentioned that he thought I looked like Anita Ekberg with my scarf tied on as a halter top with those wide-leg trousers.

Eventually, I ran into one of my friends, talent manager Shep Gordon, who took me to a bunch of fabulous parties. But first he would pull up in front of clothing stores on the Riviera in a stunning convertible, help me to run in to put on something to wear, and pay for these amazing items. Then we'd peel out to yet another—I have to admit—pretty fabulous party at someone's super-swanky waterfront pad: ancient, gorgeous specimen trees surrounding the most elegantly worn Belle Époque mansions.

It was fun making that movie, that crazy, very original *Total Recall*, for which Rob Bottin won a Special Achievement Award at the Oscars for the visual effects. This award isn't given out every year; in fact, it's been given out only sixteen times. What a genius. In fact, he is the person who taught me the Hollywood response: smile and nod and say nothing.

The whole film was nuts. I fell in friend-love with Arnold and "his lunkheads," as I called them then, while I was training my brains out a million hours a week. I was trying to figure out how the hell I was going to catch up to be even remotely believable as someone who could threaten Arnold Schwarzenegger. Yeah, that makes sense. All 128 pounds of me, beating the shit out of Arnold, in space.

So I gained a lot of weight. Drank protein powder, worked out at Easton's gym, which is a hellhole of wonder and commitment with a fan on the floor, no music, and a lot of weights and serious dudes on ancient exercise bikes staring ahead at old fish tanks.

I was 145 pounds and deadlifting wearing one of those leather belts, trunks, and a sports bra by the time we made the movie. Single-arm curling thirty-five pounds and doing karate three hours a day. But when I got to Mexico City, where we were on location, I still couldn't get my leg straight up over my head. And per the script, the infamous leg kick was choreographed straight to Arnold's face, and he is more than six feet tall.

I was terrified. I went to the gym, lightheaded, at—I don't remember—seven thousand feet or however high the altitude is in Mexico City. We shot there before, during, and after the 6.8 earthquake. My now-lifelong friend Grace Jones called me after the quaking and crashing and terror stopped, saying, "Darrrling, we're all in the barrrr, come down," in her tiger purr. I was too freaked out to get in the elevator from my thirty-ninth-floor room or too lazy to take the stairs, but not Grace and her then-boyfriend, the Danish actor and stuntman Sven Thorsen; no, they were alive and living it. In fact, rumor had it Sven was drinking Champagne out of Grace's shoe. No, I stayed in my room and commanded my floor like a soldier for two days and then worked out every day until the guys in the gym puked and then I worked out some more, and I still couldn't do that kick. I was cranked up. Obviously, I was so competitive, so tough and immeasurably determined. Thank God, or I would have killed myself in this business, just saying. Or in waitressing.

But then I had the stunt coordinator, Joel, working with me, and he was a badass. He was also super-cute and really nice, but he was killing me, pushing me as far as he could; so I pushed myself and, voilà, the night before the shoot, I kicked him in the head. I have never seen anyone more delighted by being kicked in the head.

However.

The next a.m., when I got to work, Arnold and, yes, all of the lunkheads, who now seemed just super-fit, healthy, and amazing to me—and much less lunky—were there. Sven was there, serving as Arnold's double: Sven, who was later in *Gladiator* and fought the tiger in the Colosseum. Yes, that Sven. And Arnold's trainer and mine, Joel, who I then saw standing right next to Arnold and realized that he was much shorter than Arnold, by at least my foot length. I became afraid again that I wouldn't make it to Arnold's sky-high head. The altitude suddenly kicked in.

Then Arnold asked me if I had worked with knives for the knife fight. What? "The stunt people had said I wouldn't be doing the knife fight," I told him.

"Yeah, but you should be able to do enough to cut in and out from the double," he said.

I felt like the biggest failure on earth. Oh, I would kick the crap out of him today, oh, hell, he was going to get it. I would take all of this out on Arnold, that asshole—how dare no one let me know what I needed to know, how dare I fail!

Of course, now I realize he did that to get me going. He's such a stinker. I kicked the crap out of poor Arnold. He was just covered in bruises. Lunkhead indeed, Governor Schwarzenegger—well, I'm a Democrat but I voted for him. In fact, while Arnold was governor of California, he worked with me and us at amfAR to change laws and do great work. He was a very important person in terms of understanding the HIV/AIDS crisis and doing something about it. I was impressed with his understanding of the law and how it could be used to help.

He taught me so much, about how to do my job, better than I thought I could, and how to do publicity: "Answer the question they should have asked."

Brilliant, I have to say, unless it's . . . none of anyone's business. Then I ask a question about them. He taught me that too.

So, yeah, we made the film and made it to Cannes, where I arrived with my one outfit and my dear friend Shep saved me and took me to the parties in new, beautiful party clothes for each. It seemed amazing. It was my first experience with the excess of riches on the Riviera; what did I know?

After much pleading from me—as, guess what? I made about nothin' to make that movie, next to the boys' salary—the movie's producers bought me a dress to wear to *Total Recall*'s screening. It was a black wrap Hervé Leger dress, which I still have, it is so sexy. The Gipsy Kings played at our party at the Hotel du Cap-Eden-Roc, overlooking the sea. The Rolling Stones came, and so did Eric Clapton, amid a sea of stars. My brilliant new best friend, the tiger slayer Sven, said the funniest thing I ever heard to Steven Seagal, who was always so damn mean to everyone, challenging them to martial arts duels in every inappropriate place, just as the stories go. When I worked with him on the movie *Above the Law,* he told me not to stand too close, as I was standing in his "chi."

But like my grandma Lela always said, "If you don't have something nice to say, don't say anything at all."

Kitchen-Sink Irish

I know my family sounds nuts, but this is the typical Irish-American way of growing up. They say there are two kinds of Irish: lace-curtain and kitchen-sink. We are kitchen-sink. In other words, if you have four kids and one bathroom, you piss in the sink.

Once my mother had trained my Mike and me, she hit the sofa. She had had it. She had fibroid tumors in her uterus and I'm sure the endometriosis that both my sister and I inherited and that was what disallowed us to have our own children.

There was no fancy dining room: we ate only in the kitchen. That kitchen was full of laughter and tears. It was a family kitchen. We carried the laundry up from the basement to fold it there in the winter. This is where my mother taught me to "read" cards, to know what they were without looking. One time I went to Vegas with a friend of mine, Paris Libby, who had been brought up similarly. Paris was my on-the-road stylist for the ten years of my superstardom. Paris and I have a psychic energy about what's coming. We were killing it at the blackjack tables. They asked us to leave. We laughed. Were we counting cards? Well, yeah, but we always do. Did we know what was coming up? Well, yeah, but we always do, kind of. Grow up with nuts, be a nut. I find myself counting house numbers, adding, while I'm having a conversation in the car. Doesn't mean I know where I am.

But when it came to the family table, I always knew. We played cards at that table; we were punished by being forced to sit there all night, and we did. We did our homework at that table. We sat there until the Formica was worn through.

Beautiful Thanksgiving dinners with all of the trimmings were served there, Christmas and Easter too, all of our birthdays; Mom laid it all out. Until I had three kids, or maybe until they all hit puberty at the same time, I don't think I realized how hard she worked to keep it all together. Together she kept it. Spotless, and food on the table. Watching those quarters and dimes at the same time.

Each time she or my dad saved a dime or even a nickel, it went into a mason jar toward their future. Toward a business they hoped to start once we were all grown, when they could risk it.

Of course, I didn't understand then. I had no idea what that meant or what that kind of commitment was. To each other, to their dream, and to us.

After *Basic Instinct* opened the Cannes Film Festival in 1992, I was invited by my then–dear friends Bill and Nancy to stay with them in their friends' gorgeous house on the Riviera. There I took my first tennis lesson. I was beginning to realize: this is what rich people do. What they also do, and what I finally could do and did, was pay off my parents' mortgage. I sent an anonymous money order for the seventeen thousand dollars left on their house.

I was on the tennis court when I got a phone call from my mom and dad. My mother was crying. "Did you do this?"

"Do what?" I said innocently.

"You know what," she said, still crying. My mother told me that she had gone to the bank to tell them of their error and found that someone had done this and then she'd gone to my dad's shop to tell him to take the day off. "We don't have a mortgage anymore," she had told him. "Let's go to lunch." They did, and he told her, "Get anything you want, get the other sandwich, the one that is twenty-five cents more—we can afford it." I stood there, tennis racket in hand. Yes, this is what rich people do.

But we had our own kind of wealth as children. Dinner on the table every night, everything made from scratch. Wonderful food: everything from popovers to roasts and gravy to homemade cakes and pies with fresh fruit or custards and creams. My mother canned food all summer so that we would have vegetables all winter. She made my dad breakfast every morning before he went to work or every afternoon when he worked nights. She waited up for him when he worked late. He never came home to a cold, quiet house. I remember hearing him open the door and laughing. They had a big love. She used to think up crazy things to make him laugh. She will kill me for saying this, but I remember that she wrapped herself in cellophane to greet him coming home from work late one night. I think that is hilarious. They were happily married until the day he died.

From them, from their undying love for each other, from their ability to keep it all together, and from our indentured servitude to this family machine, we all learned what it took and takes to get anything to happen. We were kith and kin, as all good Irish families are. We took our beatings without complaint and we did our work grumbling but also without complaint or there would be another beating on the other end.

Back then there wasn't time or energy for the sweetness and snuggles that my generation learned to give to our children. I see now how much my parents missed, not only by not giving that, but moreover by not receiving the depth and meaning of that kind of parent-child love. I only felt awkward hugging my mother. Now she is a hugger, a lover, a grandma. My father, before he died, also became much more affectionate; he opened like a flower.

Dad was Mother's knight; he stood when she entered the room, pulled her chair out at the table, and thanked her every night and told her how delicious dinner was.

When I started to date, I had to be home at ten o'clock. To ensure this would happen, my mother made homemade cinnamon buns, which would be coming out of the oven to be frosted at exactly ten p.m. Whoever I was dating would have me home right on time. She knew her stuff. Of course, I was grounded a week for every minute I was late. There was no messing with Joe Stone's daughters.

Once, when I ran upstairs to Dad after some kid had come on the property and scared me by looking into the living room window, he came down in his pajamas, jumped in the truck, putting his shotgun behind him in the gun rack, and drove that kid, who was by then running his ass off, right off the property. That became the hilarious dinner story for weeks to come.

Our childhood was full of big Christmases; even if the gifts were often small, they were exciting. All wrapped nicely and hidden with great secrecy, though of course we all knew where they were in the attic. As children we went up there and studied them until Dot changed the tags and put the boys' names on ours and the girls' names on theirs just to mess with us.

The attic was full of all kinds of great stuff: clothes and furniture and art stuff. I helped my dad staple fiberglass to the ceiling up there. My brother had left for the air force and I was now Dad's helper. We wore protective eyewear and gloves, but the fiberglass still cut our arms up.

By not being put in a typical gender role–playing position at home, I was able to learn a lot of traditionally male-oriented skills, such as how to make and pour concrete, and how to lay a stone wall so it didn't fall over. All of us learned how to build a house, and since we grew up in Amish country, we learned it the Amish way, building the frame and the sides and then raising them with ropes. I mowed the lawn, shoveled snow, climbed trees, and played golf. I beat up my brothers, so I didn't get beaten up. Which is not to say there wasn't an absolute rule with Dad about not hitting girls; it was just that the boys didn't think that applied to sisters until we kicked their asses.

I love to remember the day I kicked Mike's ass. That day he held me down, spit on me, and told me what to do for the last time. I waited until I saw Mom and Dad's car coming down the road—which was called Park Avenue, by the way. When they started to turn in to the driveway, which I could see from the kitchen, I ran into the living room, where Mike was sitting cross-legged on the floor in his stretchy cotton pajamas, hair in a crew cut, watching TV. I tapped him on the shoulder so he'd turn around, then punched him in the nose as hard as I could before running like hell to the driveway, screaming and crying like a psycho.

Dad grabbed me as Mike came out of the house with his nose bleeding.

"What in the hell did you do to your sister?"

"*She* hit *me*," Mike replied.

Dad said, "Well, what did you do to make her do that?"

Mike still thinks I ruined his whole life. I was seven years younger than he was. He thought he had it made until I showed up. *Women.*

Throughout our life, my brother and I have been alternately best friends and siblings who don't speak to each other. It's like that. We are speaking now and then. He lives downstairs from Dot at her house. He takes care of her sometimes.

Just like our parents did with us. They did a horrible, beautiful, awful, amazing job with us. They gave their best. They gave us everything. All of it. The full Irish.

An Education

My high school decided to send a few of us to take college classes as an experiment. First, they did a lot of tests on the upperclassmen, and we went through the sieve, a smaller and smaller group surviving each round, until five of us were left. Four boys and I were chosen to go to Edinboro University, a nearby school. I was fifteen in the beginning of this experiment, so I didn't drive yet. The college was about thirty-five or forty minutes from our little high school in Saegertown, Pennsylvania. We drove up to the university and went our separate ways according to our areas of strength. Mine was English literature first and then science, I think, as the second. As we progressed, I started to lean toward the art history of modern architecture, with golf as my sport, since golf was sort of the agreed-upon family religion, the one place we all got along. Mike was the best golfer, along with Aunt Vonne, with Dad coming in next, then me, then Kelly and Mom.

One of the boys who was going to college with us lasted only a short while, as he was on the extreme side of intelligence and did peculiar things such as trying to prove that he could eat lightbulbs by doing so right in front of us. That was the first time we learned that smarts and common sense do not go hand in hand. Walking onto a college campus at that age, the oldest of us sixteen, we were all completely overwhelmed, however—not just the lightbulb eater. There is a huge difference between fifteen and eighteen-to-twenty-two. When we went to the commissary for lunch, the room seemed gigantic, but it wasn't: we were just so little.

During this time, my high school science teacher, who was in his twenties, was hitting on me nonstop, even keeping me after school. He was the one who had administered most of the college-admissions tests. He always seemed to think I needed lots of tutoring.

I was trying to deal with all of these crazy new circumstances and at the same time pretending that it was all normal. After our college courses, we drove back to high school and went to our office, where we tutored other high school kids (I tutored algebra) or to the classrooms, where we would student-teach with the regular teacher in the room (I was helping with ninth-grade English).

This was all so fucked up. The algebra tutoring was easy and not too bad, except that it alienated me from the other kids at school, although I did get to hang out in the senior lounge, where I made friends by playing gin rummy. The English student-teaching thing was heartbreaking, as through it I discovered that at least half of these kids couldn't read. I asked them about the homework and they were clueless; so I started having them do it in class, and still they were clueless; so I asked them to open to the reading, and we would read it aloud in the room, student by student. Well, the first girl read beautifully, but it was downhill from there. There were an astonishing number of kids who simply could not read anywhere near their grade level, who had nevertheless been shoved through the system.

This is the most significant thing this experiment taught me. But I was pretty much my own educational guide from that point forward. I graduated high school and continued my college classes in the summer through to the fall. My grades in college were not exceptional. For me it had become about what interested me, what I wanted to know. I studied painting, astronomy, more golf, of course. I also did an independent study in "radio production," which involved meeting my teacher on Tuesday mornings with something interesting to talk about over breakfast at the local IHOP. He was brilliant and elderly, and I think unwell. This was the class I worked the hardest for, because he was so kind to me. I researched subjects near and far so that I would be entertaining, engaging, and create some kind of interchange that he might not hear every day.

He bought me huge breakfasts, which would have been expensive for me then, and hard to come by, and we talked for at least two hours at a time. I learned more from him than I had from most of my teachers.

I had a boyfriend off campus who was older than I was, somewhere in his late twenties, my brother Mike's roommate in Findley Lake, New York. If you don't know where that is, it's the area in the movie *Unstoppable* where the train driven by

Denzel Washington hits a horse trailer stopped on the tracks. That whole film was shot around where I grew up and went to school. It was all very *Deer Hunter.*

John was my brother's pot-dealing partner. He was so bright and very funny and looked, I would have to say, quite a bit like John Malkovich: prematurely bald, with glasses, a fabulous physique, and that brain. He was a history buff, always reading, and took me to the record store constantly, turning me on to great jazz. He took me to see Count Basie in a hotel ballroom for my eighteenth birthday. We had a blast: we danced all night, and I ended up sitting on the Count's piano bench watching him play before it was over. It remains one of the best nights of my life.

John taught me to drive a dirt bike and we would take them out to the place where they were building the new highway and jump the little hills where the new road was being put in. When I was able to become airborne coming off the backside, he invited me to Tito's for dinner. That was a spectacular moment for me. The chef and owner had been the chef of the president of Yugoslavia, and for our little neck of the woods that was quite fancy. We dressed up and went to dinner and when we arrived, the chef was playing a xylophone. Somehow, John found a way to make a grand adventure out of everything.

When we went trout fishing, he brought lunch with a crystal decanter of wine and two goblets; we would consume the wine while smoking dope, standing in our hip waders, fishing in the clear mountain streams. During the week I went to school and he did whatever he did, and on the weekends, and eventually more often, I would drive up to the house to see him and my little beagle puppy, Bogie.

John made a place for me to paint on the back porch. We cooked, he read, I painted while we listened to jazz.

Eventually Mike decided to get into the cocaine business. John didn't want to do that. I certainly didn't want him to, nor did I want to be involved with my brother's shenanigans. It got really scary really fast. People were sitting at the kitchen table at their place doing huge piles of cocaine and I was trying to go to college and pretend this all wasn't happening. Mike bought a Rottweiler, a red one he named Saber. This sleek young dog licked a big pile of cocaine off the coffee table and went wild. It was terrifying to me, though everyone else seemed to think it was funny. There were shotguns by the front door and some random guy fell unconscious in the living room.

Suddenly my brother became someone I didn't know. He overdosed and passed out in my little two-bedroom shack near school. My roommate and I literally had to put him on our backs and drag him across the tiny living room all night to keep him conscious. He went from bad to worse. Car accidents, police arresting him, hospitalizations, more police—until finally the FBI captured him the day before Christmas in a hotel just over the New York state line. In New York the laws were considerably harsher, and he had kilos of cocaine. The FBI arrested him on live television and put him in the Attica state prison for fifteen years to life.

Suddenly our family was being threatened by people who didn't want Mike to tell who he was working for and by those who did. There were consequences to each scenario. He was finding his way in jail. He became a scribe for those who needed letters written to their loved ones. He is a wonderful poet and has extraordinarily gorgeous handwriting that matches his poetic nature. He is a spoken-word artist now who works with the Rolling Stones' producer. Ah, but then.

Then he was a kid who joined the air force at seventeen, became a crew chief jet mechanic at the Dover Air Force Base. There, where the headless bodies of our soldiers were coming back from Vietnam in the empty missiles. The Viet Cong took heads, we took ears, in case you didn't know about the trophy part of war.

One day when my brother was in the air force, he was up on a hydraulic lift working on his car, and then jumped down, catching his wedding ring on the trunk latch and ripping his finger off. He ended up in the amputee ward with the vets coming in from Vietnam. He got gangrene and nearly lost his hand and part of his arm. He saw too much. These guys were smoking marijuana and using heroin to cut the extraordinary phantom pain they were struggling with. This is where he began to see the drug world unfurl. This, I imagine, is where his life changed from that of the country boy with the all-American ideals to the guy who ended up in Attica.

When he finally got out after a few years, he had to do ten years of parole. Then he came to Los Angeles and moved in with me. I was just starting to work in films, had just done *Total Recall*. Mike would have loved to work, but no one would hire an ex-felon. He did his time, terrible time in a terrible place.

And now? His life was ruined, all of it. There was no paying his dues. The dues went on, go on forever. This will break a man. I've seen him become sober so many times and do so well, and struggle to be a right guy. And fall apart again. But to what end? Who will respect this man? My brother falls again. He is up now, just launching his album and doing a film in Brazil. His album is not just his story but the stories of other men like him. It is beautiful and valuable. But will it be enough to pay those dues? Can we as a society allow those dues to be paid? Can he as a man ever re-find himself?

My father never stopped loving him or working with him or believing in him. I think that is what good men do. They grow and learn.

Life has a way of answering our questions and teaching us while we teach others. Yet those who dare are judged. We are named, named names that carry unending responsibility and meaning, and that meaning is different to everyone who speaks those words and different to everyone who must be those things. What is a criminal, a movie star, a carpenter, a CEO of a charitable foundation? What is a poet, a humanitarian, a hunter, a sufferer of lupus? What is a big brother, a bitch, a husband, a sister? What is a hero, a failure, a leader, a winner?

Life has answered a lot of these questions for me. Life has in fact posed a lot of these questions for me. In Buddhism there is a thing called a koan, where a question is used to provoke great doubt. Everyone gets one in their life. They make you or break you. Mine both broke me and made me again. I have found that in these cases sometimes the question is the answer.

Work

There was no question about working when I was growing up. Everyone worked. Of course, my dad didn't want my mom to work; he was old-school and he didn't want her to do more than she was already doing: raising four kids and cleaning our giant farmhouse. She also helped him clean, butcher, cure, and store the deer, rabbit, birds, and fish that he hunted for our food for the colder months. But for the rest of us, work it was.

Mike started with his paper route when he was very young, and I found a way to sell pots and pans door-to-door for some extra spending money and to give my mom new kitchenware. I got her an electric frying pan and griddle, which was Teflon and a huge hit on the weekends. I would sell anything door-to-door that I could find in magazines.

I also did the drawing contests from *Reader's Digest*, only to come home and find a guy in our living room, talking to my mom about sending me to art school. The problem was that I had lied about my age, as one had to be a teenager to enter, and I was only eleven. So when I waltzed in the door, clearly not a teenager, no one was happy to see me: surprised but not happy.

I apparently had some talent—or enough for the art school shyster to come out to try to con my mom—but not enough to enroll an eleven-year-old.

I saw a lot of those type of guys come to our door over the years: Mary Kay salesmen, encyclopedia salesmen, vacuum cleaner salesmen, those guys that deliver cleaning products monthly. My mom let most of them pitch her. I think it gave her someone to talk to, and she was so pretty I'm sure they liked talking to her too. She had been such a young bride, after all, and she had that dark hair, white skin, those husky blue eyes, and that red lipstick that I still copy. But our house was spotless; she didn't need their products.

She did, however, decide to become an Avon lady about the time I was twelve or thirteen, and that was cool because I could "borrow" her lipstick samples and put those awful coral lipsticks on at the bus stop. Oh, I thought I was so fancy and grown-up when I whipped one of those little white tubes out of my pocket, which I did with great flourish and pride. My mom was a working woman and she was reading *Fear of Flying*—I knew because it was hidden on top of the fridge. She was also starting to read Gloria Steinem. Now, that was interesting. Because I read; I read everything I could get my hands on.

So I started leaving books around for her to find too. I left *The Prophet,* and some other little crumbs. I left *Cosmopolitan* magazine on the coffee table. No words were said, but we were becoming liberated, silently and carefully, without a discussion.

She did, however, take me to see *Georgy Girl,* starring Lynn Redgrave, at the drive-in. I'll never forget watching Lynn as

Georgy try on new ways of discovering herself on-screen, only to decide she liked herself the way she was.

As soon as I was old enough to get any job at all, I did, and she drove me. I worked at McDonald's as a fry girl, and a shake girl, a pie girl, and then a counter girl. The manager, who seemed so old to me then, was probably pushing thirty and harassed me constantly—to the point that I eventually quit, or he fired me, or both. I got a job at the Bob's Big Boy a bit farther out of town. I was a pie girl: I put the prepacked gunk into the pie shells; then I was a busboy—there weren't bus gals back then. I worked my way up to becoming a waitress, now trusted with the clients.

That went great: I loved the challenge. I couldn't have enough tables. I loved seeing how many plates I could balance up my arms, and I loved speeding around the restaurant and being good at it. Even though the tips were often a quarter or fifty cents. They liked me, and soon I became the head waitress at night and the nighttime manager.

At the same time I was keeping up my studies and participating in county beauty pageants. I was allowed to do these pageants because they were scholarship things. Funnily enough, John Bruno, a high school classmate who played the drums at one such pageant to my dramatic recitation of the Gettysburg Address—it was 1976, centennial year—would end up being the prop guy on the Ryan Murphy series I recently did, *Ratched*. I teased him, and flirted with his son.

My parents would go up to their hunting cabin in the woods of Pennsylvania for the weekends, taking Kelly and Patrick with them, and leave me home by myself. (Mike had already joined the air force.) I was seventeen. They would drive down to the pay phone to call me when I was supposed to be home from work. I would get home in time to answer their call. At first this worked out great.

I had gone to the prom with my best friend and fellow student-lounge card player, Ray Butterfield. He had a big red fro and was such a great kid. He was on the football team, and my friendship with him helped me to be friends with people at high school, since I was—as I still am—a bit socially awkward. So going to the prom with Ray was just so much fun. He wore a baby-blue tux and I, in my enthusiasm to look fabulous, sat in front of a sun lamp and was pink, with Sun In–dyed sort of orangey blond hair and a peach dress. Basically, I was many shades of pink and peach. We were a seventies dream couple. Our picture is adorable.

A few months after the prom, I came home from work late, as I usually did, about one o'clock in the morning. I spoke to my parents but I just couldn't settle. I washed off the day and came back downstairs and sat pressed tightly against the end of the sofa. I was filled with anxiety. I didn't turn on the TV, as our three channels would be at the end of their day anyway. I sat there all night without moving. All night, it felt as if I never breathed.

Suddenly, as the sun began to rise, the phone rang, startling me. I ran to the kitchen and answered the yellow wall phone. It was Ray's mother. "Sherry," she said, and began to weep uncontrollably.

"Is he dead?" I asked.

"Yes" was all that she said. I hung up the phone. I called the police up in Tionesta, where my parents were, and asked them to go and get them. They came home.

Ray had been riding home on his motorcycle and a drunk driver had hit him. They could tell by the skid marks on the highway: where the driver had struck him, how the driver hadn't stopped to help him. Ray had only a broken jaw, but since the drunk driver hadn't stopped to check, to help, Ray had choked to death on his own blood at seventeen years of age. Alone in the night, while I sat on the couch, panicking for him, knowing the unknown, feeling the fear, wondering what was holding me so tightly.

I attended his funeral, and I went to the front to talk. Our prom picture was in Ray's breast pocket. Suddenly all of his friends, the whole football team, filed in and stood silently against the back wall of the funeral home, arms crossed, heads bowed. Then they looked up at me, waiting for me to say something.

I was impaled by their youth, their expectancy, the nothingness I had to give. I stood there, lost.

Then I stepped down and walked out of that funeral home and down the street, saying nothing, as nothing could be said. Nothing at all.

I would go on to join Mothers Against Drunk Driving as soon as it was formed in 1980.

About twenty-five years later, I was called to jury duty for a case against a third-time drunk driver who had hit someone. The defendant arrived in a suit he had obviously slept in: he was unshaven, unclean, hungover. When the judge asked me during voir dire if there was a reason I couldn't serve on the jury, I said yes, as the man was obviously still drunk, still hungover. She tried to talk me down. There was no talking me down. There is no talking me down. This is a crime I cannot understand. Take a taxi, for God's sake. Take an Uber now. In my opinion, no car should start without a built-in breathalyzer that says you are sober enough to start the car. I will never recover from seeing my seventeen-year-old prom date with our prom picture in his pocket in that casket, with the lost look of all of his friends standing by. Never.

I went back to work. I met my first serious boyfriend, D. He was an engineer on the Erie-Lackawanna. For our little town he was quite successful. I was almost eighteen when we met, and he was twenty-three. My parents thought that was a huge age difference, but he was a terrific guy and they liked him. They might have liked him less if they knew that I was coming home to answer their calls and going right back out again.

D would drive me to where the old road used to be before the dam was built. He knew exactly where that road was. So we would drive through the trees and into the water very slowly, and then go all the way out into the middle: I mean *right* into the middle; it looked like we were parked in the middle of the lake with the water just edging up to door-level. D would park, open the doors, put on music, pull out a couple of cocktail glasses, make us a couple of drinks, and fire up a joint. And we would sit out there in the moonlight and talk and hang out. It was just magical. I was very impressed with him.

He would have bought groceries for the weekend. As we got close to my parents' house, he would turn out his headlights so the neighbors wouldn't see us come in and tell my folks later. I would run like hell down the driveway and open the garage door, and he would turn off the engine and coast into the garage. Then we would grab the groceries and we would tuck in for the weekend.

It was so much fun.

Of course, despite all of *this* planning, you have to consider the extreme country background we both came from. And my sexual inexperience.

When I went back to college full-time in the fall and just started plumping up, no one—not my family, not me—thought about why. Except D, who one day asked me if I might be pregnant.

"*What?*"

"Well, I don't remember you having a period lately and you are gaining a bunch of weight. . . ."

"Holy cow."

He took me for a pregnancy test and yes, I was pregnant. "How is this possible?" I asked.

He turned the question around: "Didn't *you* do something?" He thought I had. And so forth.

Well, it was too late for all of that now. Despite the *Roe v. Wade* decision in 1973, abortions were difficult to get in Penna, especially at my age. What were we going to do? I was the county beauty queen and an exceptional student; we were not in the marriage moment of our lives. We were—or I should say *I was*—freaked out. He said to give him a few days and he would figure it out.

He came back and said he had found a clinic in Ohio that we could go to and he would take me. He got time off and we drove to Ohio. I looked so much younger than my age and I had no idea how long I had been pregnant. I heard the doctors talking about me in the next room. They also had no idea what to do with me. They didn't know if I really was eighteen or if I was less than three months pregnant. They were struggling with their ethical decision. They too were young, and this was a tough call. I was devastated, as my whole life hung in the balance.

They came out as a group and decided that I could have the surgery. I was too scared and shocked to know what to do. D took care of me and took me in. He drove me back to school that day. I think I fell asleep or passed out, and when I came to, I was bleeding all over the place and far worse than I should have been, but this was a secret and I had no one to tell. So I stayed in my room and bled for days. I was weak and scared and then just weak.

When I finally came out of it, I took all of the bloody sheets and clothes and torched them in a burning barrel at school and showered in the shared showers in the dorm and went back to class. I refused to talk to D ever again. I was too scared, ashamed, traumatized, fractured, tormented, and, most important, uneducated about everything, to move.

Eventually, a local Planned Parenthood opened, and I went for proper birth control and some counseling. This, above all else, saved me: that someone, anyone, could talk to me, educate me. No one ever had, about anything.

My mother tells me now that no one talked to her either. No one told her about her periods, about birth control: nothing at all. When she started her period, she was told only that there was Kotex in the closet. At school a boy told her she would bleed to death. She became pregnant at sixteen by my father and that was the end of her childhood. The end of her choices.

I continued to work, to study. My work ethic became stronger. My desire to help other women became stronger. Because I came from survivors, I was always proud of the work I took.

I got my first big job at school: I ran a pool hall and was the short-order cook. At first, they didn't think a girl could handle it. But I was a pretty good pool player and knew my way around kicking some ass with a pool cue, and I could hustle up a meal in record time. Still can.

I loved working in that pool hall: I could study at the bar when it was slow and feed my roommate too. We had a great apartment. We had very separate lives, but we were working our asses off to get through.

Then I got offered a better job: to waitress the night shift and manage the Holiday Inn restaurant. This came with benefits other than the upscale environment. As this was the only decent place to stay in our college town, all of the acts that came through stayed there. So I held the kitchen for them and sometimes got to talk to them after their shows. I distinctly remember talking to George Benson after his concert; I was such a jazz fan and had written a paper about him. This was inspiring.

However, for me the best was the local priest who would come up often for drinks at evening's end. He was so brilliant and such a great conversationalist. I have found over the years of traveling that religious leaders are so often the most educated and thoughtful conversationalists and those I tend to sit with at hotels at the end of the night. Whether Catholic, Protestant, Jewish, Muslim, Buddhist, or whatever: when one is dedicated to the study of faith and education, one is generally the most illuminated, as long as the commitment to kindness is still up front.

I had always wanted to pursue a career in the film business. The movies excited my brain. I thought originally that I would be a director, having no idea that women were not invited into this branch of the biz. Of course, once folks got a look at me, they decided for me. I was just happy to find a way to ease out of where I was and to find any movement toward my own goals, so I agreed with everyone about anything that sent me in that direction.

But it wasn't until my brother got into such hot water with the drug dealing and the subsequent violence that it brought upon all of our lives that my parents considered any of this a viable consideration for me. Prior to this, the idea of wasting my mind on such a frivolous profession would have sent my father through the roof. Then, however, with the incredible violence with which Mike was arrested and his business partners and their spouses were arrested, beaten, killed, and so forth, my parents began to believe that they should get me out of town. I of course agreed, for those reasons and my own.

My mother saw Eileen Ford on *The Merv Griffin Show*, and suddenly this became something, someone she could relate to. Modeling seemed like a real job, with a boss, not ephemeral, like acting, which was what I wanted. Did she call Ford Models, did we make an appointment, did we know where or what to do? Nope, not at all. We packed our old suitcases and went to visit my crazy aunt in New Jersey.

We looked up the agency in the yellow pages. We took the bus to the city and went over there—for two hicks it was rather amazing that we even found the place and saw Eileen. She told me she would like to throw me down the flight of stairs I had just come up and bounce the fat off of my ass. But that she would take me. I didn't know what to make of that.

Mom—or Mother, as I called her then—and I decided to see a couple of other agents. We went to see Wilhelmina Cooper at her eponymous agency. She was incredibly generous and explained exactly why Eileen wanted me and why she wanted the country-girl fat off. She had a silk scarf on her head, and I would soon discover that she was dying of cancer.

She treated me with so much kindness and so much dignity, and gave me great advice. I signed with Eileen and moved in with one of her agents.

Role Models

When I left home to move to New York, my dad gave me this one-inch little square cutout from the paper with Babe Ruth's stats on it. It said he had struck out so many times, but he had one of the highest batting averages. Dad said, "Just make sure you keep getting up to bat, honey."

Well, I do love baseball, and who doesn't love the Babe? I carried that piece of paper with me everywhere and it's still in my library today. And I have struck out a lot! But my batting average isn't too bad, and it's improving all the time.

My dad taught me the meaning of a work ethic. He worked swing shift in a factory an hour from home when we were little. That is where one week you work first shift, from morning till about five in the evening; then the next week, you work after-noons from about two till eleven p.m.; then the next week, you start at eleven p.m. and work until morning. Then the next week you start over. He did that for years.

That is how I learned to bust my ass. That is how I learned about respect.

I respect my dad.

I also really love my dad, but that warm feeling came later. Quite a bit later.

All through grade school, I remember waiting every night for him to come home, scrunched up at the top of the stairs, hovering on the scarlet carpeting my mother so wanted to have. We had little money for furniture, yet somehow she made the most interesting choices. Just one big, curved black Persian lamb–looking sofa for the living room and a mid-century pale-wood *Jetsons*-style coffee table with golden legs. A yellow faux-leather ottoman in front of the fireplace, and of course the console TV with its three glorious stations. And the scarlet carpet where I waited for my father to come home from second shift in the Erie forge shop, where they gave him an engraved brass lighter when he retired. With his hour's drive home, he arrived near midnight.

I waited to see what my mother would do. Would she greet him with love, with jokes, with a late supper, or would there be the irritated stories of what I hadn't done well enough, right enough? I had to know, to be ready. For if I had failed, the energy would build until my father would come up the steps and grab me and either yank me down with him or throw me down in front of him. After which I could redo my first failed attempt at washing the car if the hubcaps weren't shining, or mowing the lawn if I had missed a spot, or washing the floor, or whatever the case may be. The neighbors often came calling to see if there was a catastrophe.

This, of course, was better than when he was on first shift

and my mother would stand, back to the room, facing the sink, as I was dragged through the kitchen to the basement to get the crap strapped out of me with a belt. I wised up to that pretty quick and started bathing and putting on my nightgown and pink fuzzy robe very early, as I could put a big, soft paperback book in my underpants and not get found out.

It continued until I was so sure I didn't do what I was being punished for that I lost all fear, all concern—in fact, all feeling. I simply saw my father as weak. He yelled for me at the bottom of the stairs to come down. She was standing beside him. I came down, as slowly as I possibly could, never losing eye contact with either of them. I walked up to him and said, "What's the matter—do you need to hit me some more to feel like a man?"

I was fourteen. He started to cry. I told him I didn't love him. That I had never loved him. That I would never love him. I was so cold, so still. He was so heartbroken. He never hit any one of us again.

I was free. From them both. From then on, I was my own guide.

That didn't stop me from continuing to come home, continuing to argue with him, and continuing to need his approval. After all, he was my dad. I would come home from New York City—and later, still, I would come home from L.A.—and argue with them about politics, the Vietnam War, Anita Hill. Oh, I was on fire about Anita Hill. I would refuse to wear a bra. One time, my father said I couldn't come to the dinner table without a bra, so I went upstairs and put my mother's bra on over my peasant blouse, came down, and sat at the table and said, "Okay, now can we eat?"

But when I was a young model in New York, I was making my own decisions. I was no longer having amazing conversations with my father where he used to make me explain why I wanted to see each and every film in order to be allowed to go. Why I cared about each and every idea. Even if he vehemently disagreed, he respected me enough to fight it out with me. But now we weren't talking about every single thing.

As a model, I was often called in to do the "difficult" jobs. I guess they too thought I was the smarter, tougher one. Those jobs where they thought the guy might be tough, or the client hard to deal with. I worked with the Buf-Puf client who put me in a light box: a small box the size of my body lined entirely with lights, with a dish of water in front of me; I was meant to take the sponge out of it and show it to the camera near my face. She just kept telling me a thousand ways to say "Buf-Puf": accent on the "Buf" or on the "Puf," whatever—she kept drilling me as if I were an object in the box. And for her I was. A million-degree box, with an assistant putting cold towels on my back so I didn't pass out.

I did jobs with famous men who arrived drunk, and with famous men who arrived sober and were terrific and with whom I am friends today, like Bruce Willis, who was spectacular and funny and kind.

I did jobs where I had to say things like "slimtintlipgloss," while landing a set-up bounce-off-a-couple-sides pool table shot. They brought in a billiards expert to teach me the shot.

I was smeared head to toe with dark Egyptian makeup mixed with coffee, with someone wiping the bottoms of my feet to keep me from suffocating from the mixture as I walked around the pool in a bikini for Coppertone. "Get a good reaction," I'd say, and the waiter fell into the pool.

I modeled bathing suits in winter at Jones Beach and furs in summer on Seventh Avenue. I wasn't a runway model: too short and too curvy. Or, in my mind: too fat and not *It*. But I was a "special bookings" girl from Ford. We were at the front of the book and we did faces and commercials and made a decent buck—and we got in free at Studio 54. In those days, I made five grand a day. Sometimes twice.

Until the scar on my neck didn't work out.

When I was fourteen, I was breaking a wild horse barefoot in the upper yard while my mom was hanging sheets on the clothesline. That damn horse took off with me. It was bucking and rearing, snorting and spinning. I was fighting this bitch of a horse, for, after all, I would make twenty-five bucks when we sold her later, broken and a pet for a country family.

I didn't realize we were heading for the wet sheets on the line until the line hit my neck and my feet slid through the stirrups. I couldn't get out and I couldn't get that dang horse to settle down. It began to rear again, and Dot just looked up at the situation—this giant rearing horse, her daughter being decapitated—and pushed its chest with some kind of dynamic maternal strength. She pushed it back and away and my right leg fell out of the stirrup and I fell off and it began to drag me. Dot grabbed my leg and freed me and stepped back, spent.

I got up and walked into the house and looked in the oval

mirror in the living room, the one over the old wooden stereo with the built-in speakers. My neck was hanging open, wet and ripped from one ear to the other. There was plasma rolling down the front of my shirt. It was a gigantic fucked-up mess of drastic proportions. There was no simple way to handle this—that we knew, but not much more.

Dot stood in the doorway, staring at me. Then she quietly turned and walked to the kitchen and called my dad at the golf course. He was already walking in. He knew. As parents do. He skidded into the driveway in our old Chevy as I sat on the worn green leather sofa in the den, not moving, looking at my hands.

They took me to the hospital. No one knew what to do, so they did nothing, for hours. Finally, my father grabbed a doctor by the lapels and threw him into the room where I was waiting, bleeding and silently falling apart on a gurney. The doctor slid in and hit the wall at the far end of the room.

"Are you a surgeon?" Dad demanded.

Yes.

"Well, then, sew her up," my dad said, and walked out.

This was not a sew job. The doctor had turned white. He just looked at fourteen inches of meaty, torn-up kid neck and then looked up at me. He cleaned the wound and butterflied it together. He did not know how to do plastic surgery or how to sew a neck, a movable piece of the body. My neck looked like I had a red, then pink, then white rope tied around it. That is how it healed. People used to say the strangest things to me about it. Not any of them nice or funny. Though many of them were "just a joke."

I have had several attempts at plastic surgery on my neck

over the years. It looks okay now, and most people don't seem to notice it. I think it's because I don't care about it on most days, and once you survive things, over time, well . . . I personally feel proud of my scars. Even the ones that no one can see.

When I was still modeling, I would come home from New York City or Paris or Rome and my father would be furious, still so angry that I "threw away an education to flounce around the world." He once said to me, "I suppose you think you're pretty chick." He meant to say, I suppose, "You think you're pretty chic." But as he was self-educated, he had pronounced it incorrectly.

I took that and ran: "Yes, Dad, I think I'm pretty chick." And went to my room thinking he was pretty stupid. He thought he was losing me, and I was being an asshole, not at all realizing how scared he was about this big scary world.

He is gone now, but in my family when someone is being a jerk, we still ask if they think they are "pretty chick." It gets the best laugh of all.

It took so long for my dad to get what I was doing, even when I brought home my tax return to prove I had made more money than him. It wasn't about the money. It was about my smarts. My dad had had plans for my smarts.

What happened to his mother, denied her inheritance because of her sex, haunted him. My father was adamant that this would never happen to me.

My dad saw forward to a world where women mattered. He saw a world where I would matter, and he thought my industry would just shit on me like it had every other woman, women who ended up dead, abused, and uncared for. He was right: this wasn't architecture or engineering, careers he had hoped for for me; this was dangerous.

He was right. It was dangerous. But I was Joe Stone's daughter, and he had taught me that if you want respect, you have to demand respect. Not ask for it, not hope for it, but *demand* it. Now, that didn't always go down too well: I got fired, got blackballed here and there. Got talked about, laughed at, and ultimately, when I did *Basic Instinct,* written off as a sex star. As if.

Try playing a serial killer, a sociopath, with a great director and a superstar like Michael Douglas and make it work, and then tell me it was all because you showed your body.

But first I had to make it into the movies. First I had to get in the door.

I got a call from my friend Riccardo Bertoni, who was an extras casting agent. He said that he knew that there was a call for a Woody Allen movie, and I should go. I was twenty, still in New York, trying to book modeling work by going out on "go-sees." I would take my book of photos from other jobs or that photographers had taken of me and show up for an audition and hope someone would hire me. Getting around New York City is expensive in taxis and awful on the subways, and at that point, on some rough days, I was still looking in pay phones for extra change. I decided to buy some used roller skates and skate to my appointments, an easy way to get the fat off and a quick way to get there.

So when Riccardo called, I skated over there as fast as I could and got in line. Once at the front, I handed my head shot to the casting lady, who turned and handed it to someone seated behind her in what looked like a bus shelter. He whispered something to her, and she said, "Woody would like you to sit down." She stepped aside and there he was.

I sat next to him and he said absolutely nothing to me for about ten or fifteen minutes. Of course I was paralyzed with fear and said nothing either. I just got up and skated away. But I got a call that I had been cast as an extra and to meet the next day wearing all white at a school gymnasium downtown.

I brought my usual bag of books and sat with a couple hundred other extras and hung out. At some point Michael Peyser, the production manager, came out and told me, "The girl who was supposed to play a part didn't show up and Woody wants to meet you to talk about you playing the part."

I was shocked, to say the least. "When?" I stammered.

"Now," he said, and left without much more.

Eventually Woody came out. I was reading a children's book about infinity; explaining infinity to a child is an interesting concept to me. When Woody came out, he seemed to think so too, and we talked for about half an hour. Then he left and Michael came back and said that I had gotten the part and would start immediately.

This was both good and terrifying. The other extras were looking at me with a combination of wonder and hostility. I was overwhelmed by the attention. They hustled me off to wardrobe and began to dress me in a skintight white Marilyn Monroe dress. I was so embarrassed. I had already been told how fat I was and now I was in a tight white dress with all of those country pounds showing everywhere. But the costumer loved the dress, the makeup people were loving it all, and the hairdresser could not have been nicer to me and put a real gardenia in my hair.

I went to the set and Woody put me on the train to do the sequence in *Stardust Memories*. He told me to kiss the window, which I did. He looked at Gordon Willis—the genius cinematographer who shot all three of the *Godfather* movies and many of Woody's amazing films, including *Manhattan*, which was so beautiful—and they just laughed. Then Woody came over to the window and leaned in and said, "No, I want you to kiss the window like you are really kissing *me*." Well, I really laid one on that window.

I was so happy on that set, and after a few days, they—Gordon and Woody—asked me if I was happy there. I said I was. They said I seemed like a natural, and though they couldn't match my usual modeling fees, they thought I would be good in the movie if I wanted to stick around for a couple of weeks. I said I would love that so much. And they wrote up my part a bit.

This was it. This was the beginning. I had inched open the door of my dream world.

Now I had to move to Hollywood and get in the ring.

Basic

I had, by virtue of having had a criminal brother who lived upstairs from my boyfriend, the intellectual pot dealer, somehow prepared myself for Hollywood. Not everyone's Hollywood, I suppose, but certainly the movie business as we met each other.

I was so shy when I got here. I wore all black clothing, only black, all of the time. My neighbors asked me why I always wore black and I told them I was like Johnny Cash. I lived in south Beverly Hills in a triplex condominium. It was so beautiful, with a garden on the side. My neighbors in back of me were Secret Service agents, brothers from a frozen-food family. They had folding chairs in their apartment; they were there for only a few days at a time. They wore suits and golf hats. I loved that. We got such a kick out of one another. They told me that if I needed anything to just yell out the window, that they could hear if I dropped my keys.

One night after I came in, I could smell aftershave in my front hall. I backed out of the apartment and knocked on their door. They went through my place like James Bond, in only their underwear, dress shirts, ties, and golf hats. Yes, and black socks. There was no one there, but I felt so damn safe. Had there been someone there? Who knows? I was freaked out, and they were awesome.

Where I came from, guys with guns handled things. This was different but the same. It seems on point that I would make it playing sociopaths and a gangster's wife, though neither of those things had much to do with me.

But that was later. When I first came to Hollywood, I was still striking out a lot. Almost getting cast and then not. I knew this fellow who we all thought was a funny guy, a smart guy— interesting but really, really cheap. We used to tease him about how cheap he was. One day he said to me, "Sharon, you get so close on every project you go up on but you always come in second. You really need a great acting teacher. I know this man who is so amazing that if he doesn't completely change your life, not just your acting, your *life,* I will pay for all of your lessons."

Well, we all thought this was hilarious, this friend being so cheap, of course. So I said I would go to his guy.

And that guy changed my life.

That guy, Roy London, ended up teaching a lot of us. Not just me: Brad Pitt and Robert Downey Jr. and Forest Whitaker and Geena Davis and Garry Shandling, and oh, and the list goes on. That amazing, lovely man was such a special, dear teacher in the truest sense of the word. He passed away way more than twenty-five years ago now, and it amazes me still how I continue to learn from him. I can be standing in a drive-way waiting for someone and suddenly be struck with a deeper understanding of something from a class years ago. Good teachers are like that. They are few and far between. I am and will be eternally grateful that Roy was in my life.

The lesson that sticks with me the most was from the last class I took.

Roy had called me up and said, "You have graduated—you don't have to come back."

I panicked. "But I'm not done—I haven't gotten it."

He said, "You have played every woman's part. There is nothing left to do."

So I said, "Then I need to come back and play the men's parts."

He reluctantly agreed.

I came back and we started. Actually, he first had me do an Oscar Wilde piece for two women; he was still unsure that I hadn't simply lost my mind and that I might not with some convincing go away. When it was clear I was there to stay, he assigned me Mamet's *Glengarry Glen Ross*. I came back with a ferocious determination. His notes to me after the first performance were to go home and not work on it for a week. For me a near impossibility.

I did as I was told. Although I cried a lot that week.

I came back and, with great insouciance, did the scene. I ripped it up. The class stood still. I had found my place. Roy was simply stunned. I will never forget the look on his face as he slowly turned to the class and then to me and said, "Well, what have we learned?"

And I said, "That I am enough."

He said, "You have graduated, class dismissed."

Sometimes it is the part of us that is not like others that makes us special, that is our talent. I would go so far as to say sometimes it is the antisocial piece, the part that makes it hard to be the hit of the party, that makes us wonderful. It was very hard for me to get to that part and make it my own.

Chuck, my manager at the time, had told me that no one would hire me because everyone said I wasn't sexy. I wasn't, as they liked to say in Hollywood at the time, "fuckable."

I was still so shy and introverted. But Roy kept badgering me. Roy would ask me, "If you keep leaving your sexuality at the door, how do you expect to play anyone at all?"

Six weeks later I was cast in *Basic Instinct*.

That makes it sound easier than it was. It was not easy. Chuck had to break into the casting director's office with his credit card and steal the script so we could read it, as no one would give it to us. I knew right away that I wanted to play that part. Chuck then called the director, Paul Verhoeven, every day for seven or eight months to get me a screen test. I had already done *Total Recall* with Paul, but Michael Douglas didn't want to test with me. Hey, I was a nobody compared to him, and this was such a risky movie. So Paul tested with me, and kept playing my test after those of everyone else who had tested.

Eventually, after they had offered the part to twelve other actresses who had turned it down, Michael agreed to test with me.

The test is online. You can watch it if you want.

Michael and I are friends now. He taught me so much. He has been such a profoundly important human rights activist, and I admire him so much. He isn't afraid to play the villain; he'll say, "It's the best part—you can do whatever you want," and then he laughs that fabulous laugh, which tells you that he knows exactly where the line is.

I did a movie in Italy a while ago. The director told me to do something and I said, "Women don't act like this anymore."

He said, "Why?" and I said, "We respect ourselves."

His only response was "Next time get a mother who loves you."

I wasn't shocked. At the time, I was convinced that my mother didn't love me. How could she? Who in God's name had taken care of her? Who had taught her how a parent should love? However, I was a woman, a grown woman. A woman who, through arduous undertakings, had learned what life had done to my mother. And he? He was a man from the generation that had done it. Like Michael, I knew where the line was, and he was over it.

I stopped working for him that day. Oh, I stayed, I finished the picture. But I made sure I gave every thought to its complete disaster. Why? You can't shame me. And you will not, should not, even consider shaming my mother.

Oh, not that the universe hasn't given pause to this concept. I mean, girl. After we shot *Basic Instinct*, I got called in to see it. Not on my own with the director, as one would anticipate, given the situation that has given us all pause, so to speak, but with a room full of agents and lawyers, most of whom had nothing to do with the project. That was how I saw my vagina-shot for the first time, long after I'd been told, "We can't see anything—I just need you to remove your panties, as the white is reflecting the light, so we know you have panties on." Yes, there have been many points of view on this topic, but since I'm the one with the vagina in question, let me say: the other points of view are bullshit.

Now, here is the issue. It didn't matter anymore. It was me and my parts up there. I had decisions to make. I went to the projection booth, slapped Paul across the face, left, went to my car, and called my lawyer, Marty Singer. Marty told me that they could not release this film as it was. That I could get an injunction. First, at that time, this would give the film an X rating. Remember, this was 1992, not now, when we see erect penises on Netflix. And, Marty said, that per the Screen Actors Guild, my union, it wasn't legal to shoot up my dress in this fashion. *Whew*, I thought.

Well, that was my first thought. Then I thought some more. What if I were the director? What if I had gotten that shot? What if I had gotten it on purpose? Or by accident? What if it just existed? That was a lot to think about. I knew what film I was doing. For heaven's sake, I fought for that part, and all that time, only this director had stood up for me. I had to find some way to become objective.

I had spent so long coming to the project that I had fully examined the character and the dangerousness of the part. I came to work ready to play Catherine Tramell. Now I was being challenged again.

I can say that the role was by far the most stretching that I had ever done in terms of considering the dark side of myself.

It was terrifying. I had walked in my sleep three times during production, twice waking fully dressed in my car in my garage. I had hideous nightmares.

During the shooting of the opening stabbing sequence of the film, at one point we cut and the actor did not respond. He just lay there, unconscious. I began to panic; I thought that the retractable fake ice pick had failed to retract and that I had in fact killed him. The fury of the sequence coupled with the director screaming, "Hit him, harder harder!" and, "More blood, more blood!" as the guy under the bed pumped more fake blood through the prosthetic chest had already made me weak. I got up, woozy, sure I would pass out.

It seemed I had hit the actor so many times in the chest that he had passed out. I was horrified, naked, and stained with fake blood. And now this. It seemed like there was no line I wouldn't be asked to skate up to the very edge of to make this film.

After the screening, I let Paul know of the options Marty had laid out for me. Of course, he vehemently denied that I had any choices at all. I was just an actress, just a woman; what choices could I have?

But I did have choices. So I thought and thought and I chose to allow this scene in the film. Why? Because it was correct for the film and for the character; and because, after all, I did it.

By the way, you probably don't recall, but my name wasn't at the top with Michael Douglas's on the poster.

Because my family was dealing with Uncle Beaner's death and couldn't come to the premiere, Faye Dunaway took me. She knew just what to do. The film had so much crazy hype that the premiere was on the lot, not at a big theater: they just could not control the crowds. We were in a big screening room; when the film ended, there was absolute silence. Faye grabbed my arm and whispered, "Don't move," and I didn't. Neither did Michael, in the seat in front of me. He looked left and right, at the producers and at Paul. Finally, after what seemed like forever, the crowd began to scream and cheer. "What now?" I said to Faye, to which she replied, "Now you are a big star and they can all kiss your ass."

Basic Instinct was my eighteenth movie. For years, I had been getting pummeled doing a bunch of crap movies and so-so television back in the day when TV wasn't king. I was thirty-two years old when I got that job. I told my agent that if they got me in that door I would get the job. I knew this was the last chance—I was aging out of the business I hadn't really gotten into yet. I needed a break.

It wasn't until we took the movie to Cannes that Michael found out I had already done all those other shit movies. He stood up and made a beautiful toast to me. That moment was so amazing; I was wearing my beach coverup as an evening gown; people had broken into my room to steal Sharon Stone's belongings. I was a star and one with no money to buy new clothes. Welcome to Hollywood, honey bun. I went upstairs at this hotel/restaurant and had the dry heaves in the toilet. My friend Shep put my feet in a bathtub of cold water and told me the new rules of what it meant to be famous and gave me a Valium.

Invisible

After I was told that I got the part for *Basic Instinct,* I was asked to come in to meet with Paul Verhoeven, as well as some other people from the production company. I was so nervous and excited I could hardly hear.

I met with Paul in the company's offices in Hollywood, then said hello to a few other people on the way down to fill out some paperwork and meet the line producer, an older, kind of dodgy man, in his messy office. He closed the door and sat down and said, "*You* were not our first choice, Karen. No, you were not even the second or the third. You were the *thirteenth* choice for this film."

He continued to call me Karen all through the making and postproduction of the movie.

I left that meeting so messed up that I got into my car in the parking lot, put on my rap music super-loud, and backed into a semi three feet behind me.

When I went to the Oscars for the very first time after making that film, I sat next to this same line producer at the Governors Ball dinner, which happens right after the ceremony. He did not call me Karen.

I had to find a certain coping mechanism to play that part, with all kinds of resistance around myself and around the film happening simultaneously. The ways that I had learned to disappear inside myself made it possible to disappear inside this character, who was as tough and smooth as the white silk scarf she wore.

When I saw the film, I not only saw that I could make myself beautiful in this way—with the top talents in Hollywood highlighting all of my best parts and hiding my flaws—I could quite convincingly cover my vulnerabilities by removing the tender, fragile self at my exterior.

It wasn't that I vowed to be this character from now on, but I *would* be less weak on the outside, less available to be eaten alive.

You see, I was still making decisions based on the experiences and scars of an eight-year-old, and those deep cuts and broken bonds of security that I had not yet actively learned to replace.

I was still faking it till I made it. I was sort of good at it. But for the first time I was asking to learn how to know something new. I was asking for the world to change. I was asking for permission to say *why*.

I was asking to be seen, and respected. I was asking to be known.

Clarence, my maternal grandfather, died when I was about fourteen. Of a heart attack, as I recall. Too hot in a closed car, they said.

I realize only now how peculiar the funeral was, since this was the first one I had been to, and with my sister and I so hoping he was actually dead and all. We approached the coffin, just to check and make sure. Now I can see in my mind's eye that all of the wooden folding chairs were empty and the people were standing in small, tight bunches with their heads down, talking low in the back of the room. No one ever took a seat, no one spoke at this funeral.

Kelly and I looked into the casket. "Is he dead?" she asked. "God, I don't know." "Touch him." "Why me?" "You're older."

So I poked him, and the bizarre satisfaction that he was at last dead hit me like a ton of ice. I looked at her and she understood; she was eleven, and it was over.

I remember having to go visit them, my mother's parents. Walking into that house, opening the screen door with my little white church gloves: even in winter the smell just hit me in the face. And even before I could see anything, the sound: the squalling and scratching, the clawing and trying to get out. It should have been warning enough for someone to know that something was wrong, just wrong. My grandparents always had near a dozen cats, and would tie them to a leg of the tub in the middle of the kitchen. Who does that? And who brings their kids there and sits at that wooden table and has tea in the stench and squalor and noise?

We tried escaping into the other room. It didn't help. That time my parents left us there while they went to the courthouse. We were there in the room with the light coming in from the windows in the way that holds the dust in the air so that you can see it floating in slow motion and you just can't breathe. The light that makes the fabric on that old green chair so bright and the texture so specific, so that every single loop of fabric is terribly clear. The piano looming in the corner, so heavy and large, with the bench pulled out just so. It made me want to cry, though no one seemed to notice over the sound of those poor cats.

I wasn't alone; there was another little girl there too, wearing her best dress—the one I had worn to the courthouse years before for my IQ tests, a perfect and beautiful velvet dress with lace and ruffles and little shiny shoes with tiny perfect socks that broke my heart in two. Those socks were so delicate and fine and quiet. She was fragile, with sandy-blond curls and little glasses and a patch over one eye. I could see them through the dust in the air as my grandfather made her sit on the piano bench. Once she turned and looked at me, or at least I think she did; I kind of remember that she tried to turn and look at me.

I felt desperate, and impaled by my desperation. The floor was a weird rose color that seemed to move almost like I was flying and yet I never, ever moved, even a little bit. Or made any sounds at all or looked out the window, but I remember the thorns on the bushes and the dirt on the windows so well. And the sound of the clock: dull and inconsistent.

I still don't believe that time exists the way it does for other people; it seems to move and shape itself as I need it to. That is such a blessing, like rain and kindness and decency and clean windows.

We never talked about it until we were in our late twenties and our mother was not there. Why had she left us alone with a monster? Kelly asked.

Our mother later said she didn't know about her father's perverse behavior toward us during our toddler and elementary years. She said she was bitterly sorry. She hated him: he, Clarence, had beaten her mother every day of her mother's life. She loved us so much, she now understood why we felt about her in all of the ways that we do. And there are so many ways that I feel.

Nothing is a big way that I have felt. Just nothing, nothing at all.

For those of us who have felt this broken piece that has left us unable to mate as others seem to do, there is such comfort in solitude. There is comfort in the alone time, I guess. Or it just seems less dangerous.

I have felt rage and indignation, and I have responded with condescension and cruelty, false kindnesses, and artificial patience toward my mother. Eventually I faced myself and stopped my relationship with her.

She wrote to me. Thoughtfully, from the heart, and with passion. She said she never knew. Though it ultimately was known what he was. She was sorry, she was penitent. She loved me. That was something deeply felt from her. Something she very much wanted me to receive. And I did receive the love. I want to feel loved by my mother and I want to cleave to that love. Whatever it is. But she didn't want to see me, and I did not want to see her. There was too much brutality that cannot be explained away. She would say she had too many appointments. I would just say nothing. I'd say I loved her too. There was a part of me that loved that part of her that wanted to love me, and vice versa.

You see, I was the witness, not the victim. The little eight-year-old witness of my five-year-old sister being robbed of her innocence. I stood, paralyzed, in that dusty, dimly lit, awful place, trapped there by a woman standing in the exit so we couldn't get out. My grandmother, who was beaten every day by the devil in the room, made a devil herself.

Of course, I realize saying I wasn't a victim here seems absurd, but it was almost like I wasn't there. It was the first time I felt myself leave my body and observe from somewhere else. I saw my grandmother standing in the doorway, blocking my exit. She was holding the fingers of one hand in the grip of the other, against the tattered, faded blue rickrack that lined her worn apron, which sagged over her sagging, tired body. She looked ahead at nothing.

From somewhere else I saw the old drab green sofa, its texture worn off here and there, just behind the piano bench, where his big, gnarled hand was on the hem of her dark-blue velvet dress, just by the white lace edging. I saw her feet dangling, her little white socks, her little chubby kid legs pushed hard down against the bench, turning red in defiance, her eyes squirting silent tears from underneath her glasses, her near-perfect braids. I looked up to the bourbon-colored violin, somehow so beautiful and out of place on top of the old broken-down upright piano, silent now, like everything and everyone. I looked out the dirty window, to the debris in the yard, the broken-down blue car, where he had put me before to show me something in his pants, where I had instead shoved myself as far away as I could, looking at the texture of the old cracked leather on the window seal, the door locked, the ashtray broken. I stared at the burned grass, the weeds, the train tracks so close to the window, until suddenly the house began to shake, the windows to vibrate, the glass to scream as the train seemed as though it would drive through the house, and I smelled myself pee on the floor. My grandmother grabbed me by the back of the neck and shoved me through the doorway.

I stood in this dank room, full of boxes and a bed without covers, a bare, soiled, stinking mattress and things, metal things, rusted things; all these things, and me, with my underwear and socks off, drying on an old radiator. Me, standing near the filthy closed window, alone in the dark.

When I don't feel well, everything tastes like this room, metallic and cold, dark and alone, and I feel ever-vigilant, that hand clamping on my neck. I wait. . . . For whom, I do not know. For what? I do not know. But I am still as a church mouse, hoping that the sound of the departing train will somehow come back for me.

My grandmother tried to make it up to us, to me and my sister. She made us homemade chocolate Easter eggs every year from scratch. And I know she saved, secretly, to do so. I couldn't explain why or how much I hated them. But then, we had to kiss Grandpa goodbye. He opened his legs where we were supposed to stand for this terrible duty and stuck his tongue down our throats.

It's a very weird thing when you're a kid and the first experience you have of death is glee and relief. And emptiness.

When I played a serial killer in *Basic Instinct* I tapped into that rage. It was terrifying to look into the shadow self and to release it onto film for the world to see. To allow people to believe that I was "like that." Even more, to let myself know that I have or had darkness within. I can say that it was and is the most freeing thing I have ever done. To engage my full self so very deeply and to free that dark angel. To know that I was angry— to know that I was so angry that I would have loved to stab Clarence to death—was incredibly freeing.

Ultimately, it also let me know that I wasn't really the stabbing type. Letting myself process that rage was magnificent, and I think letting others feel that release was a bit therapeutic for the audience. I know it's not just me.

The day *Basic Instinct* came out in theaters I hired a limo. Mimi and I started in Harlem and went to movie theaters all over NYC, from one side of town to the other, into the wee hours of the morning. We had bought two bowler derbies and wore our hair up inside and both of us wore our glasses. We watched about twenty minutes at each theater.

Harlem was my favorite. People were yelling and screaming at the screen. Cheering my character on. We were having a ball, seeing the reactions all over town. We stopped in the Upper East and West Sides, Hell's Kitchen, all the way into the Bowery. We were running in and out of theaters at various points during the film and fleeing like thieves into the day and night. And the audiences went wild, they loved this movie! It was one of the best times.

The next morning while we had a glorious, celebratory breakfast, the horrible reviews came out.

What is a critic? Someone who sees movies for free and then tells you what they think.

What is an audience? Someone who tells you how a movie makes them *feel.*

Do you have any idea how many people have watched *Basic Instinct* in the last twenty-something years? Think about it. It's about more than just a peek up my skirt, people. Wake up. Women championed that movie; men were obsessed with a woman who could make it stop. She was their favorite. But now, only now, do I go to events and there is a certain respect about that film. Oh, that film is coooooool. But when I went to the Golden Globes as a nominee in 1993 and they called my name as a glamorous finalist, everyone laughed. Well, not everyone, but enough of the room so that I was told where I sat.

I think that I am not alone in processing some pent-up female rage. It's unnerving to know that for me this rage was so controlled, I think because I was forced to control it for so long, to keep it hidden as though it were my shame. This was the nature of abuse in my era. Everything carried the heavy weight of threat. Not only to me but to those I loved or was supposed to love or whateverthefuck was going on there.

Now, my sister and I have considered speaking about what happened with our grandfather in public, but we know it would be so sensationalized. It's like when I was asked on a very lovely

Sunday-morning television show if I had had any #MeToo moments in Hollywood. Me? I'm sure they were asking out of concern, or a profound desire to assist me, not out of any sensationalistic intentions, but just to be on the safe side, I said nothing. Instead I laughed, and it went viral. Apparently, I wasn't laughing alone.

As we are learning, abuse comes in all kinds of ways and our reactions come in all ways. Generation after generation we will still be learning just how to talk about and deal with abuse without being abusive in our very discussions, sensationalistic in our interest, cruel with our concern.

All of this is not to say that my family did not present the very picture of a normal Anglo-Saxon Protestant family. We went sometimes to the Emmanuel United Church of Christ, where, other than the occasional bit of hiding in the closet and doing nothing but being quiet in the dark with a boy—which was admittedly pretty exciting for church—not much was happening. The songs were all monotone. The minister was the whitest guy alive, who my mother thought was the cutest guy alive.

This reminds me of the time I finally got her to try pot.

My mother had always been inquisitive. She decided that since all of her kids smoked pot she should understand the whole phenomenon—what it looked like, smelled like, how you rolled a joint, all of it. So Kelly and I, and maybe also my older brother, Mike, sat at the kitchen table with our mother and taught her the whole thing. Just as Mom was starting to get baked, a car turned around at the top of our driveway. Our mother panicked and threw everything on the floor, screaming,

"Oh my God, it's Reverend Ziegler!" and lunging for the air freshener. She was running around the huge farmhouse kitchen spraying us and the environs with Lysol long after the car was gone.

We used this as ammunition for years when she was going to tell on us to Dad. We would stand behind him and pretend to be smoking a joint. "Jesus Christ, you are a bunch of little bastards," she would say, laughing and chasing us with a fly swatter.

Yes, we came from poverty and violence and the kind of interior crisis that seems to happen only to the very rich or the very poor. The secret kind of violence, the quiet kind of lies. We were tough, we were Irish, we looked richer than we were. We looked like we had it together. We had pride, if nothing else.

When my dad lined up our shoes, all freshly shined, on the kitchen counter, I knew something about myself. I knew we would go on, heads held up; I knew we were survivors.

I am deeply disappointed in the lack of care that kids now show for themselves. It hurts my heart. The world is getting tougher. I wonder if they will be tough enough to survive it. We survived so much, and we still say how sweet it was then compared to now. Isn't that always the way generations after generations think? That we are leaving nothing but trouble and that no one can survive what is coming and we know why?

I think we can survive anything, everything. I think that is the secret to life. Perhaps this is also just part of the cycle of growing older: this thing that we label wisdom, which is actually just the first flicker of dementia. We too have our seasons.

There was a fad once where you could be a season. This would determine which color palette was best for you. What if instead your season was where you began? So winter wasn't automatically death? Maybe winter is your summer, so to speak. I have certainly felt in my slushy period of late. Which means others should be doing the driving in the near future. But I am not scared to be feeling that surrendering thing upon me. It feels like growth.

I do love summer. I feel like summer is coming on, like the sun might shine on me in a different way. I hope it shines on my mother differently too. I have so much empathy and compassion for her. After all, she didn't get parents at all. I so wish she too had had a mother she could talk to.

While my mother didn't mother me, per se, as I've said, she was a fabulous homemaker. We are all self-sufficient. I don't think we understood at the time that parts of our upbringing were so harsh because no one did anything at all for either of our parents. Our parents clung to each other like two survivors on the shore, ravaged after a storm. They were both shipwrecked when they met.

Neither of them had proper parents, nor homes, nor care, nor providence of any kind, nor education, nor skills. They clung to each other through all seasons.

We went through everything in our big old farmhouse in Amish country, Pennsylvania. We did it as a family. Messy with white gloves on Sunday. Isn't that just how we kitchen-sink Irish families do it?

Life is simpler even in its extreme complexities when you are poorer. We had school shoes, play shoes, and church shoes. My half of the closet and my sister's half, which was bigger than my half. It was kind of understood that she got the hanging half in the front and I got the seated half in the back, where I had a pillow and a light that my dad fixed up for me. This was my library, my den, so to speak. I liked to be in there, to read and to think. Behind the clothes, in my little cubbyhole, with a book or two.

Honestly, not much has changed. I have better real estate now. My radio gets satellite, Pandora, and Deezer. I can talk to my Alexa.

At school it was considered a given that all us girls would need secretarial skills when we grew up, so we had to take a typing class. I'm kind of a fast typist—I would like to take a brief moment to brag about that. Mostly because the typing teacher, Mr. Fletcher, was also the accounting teacher, who called me "Stone, you mental midget" in every single class in front of everyone. He said it was "only a joke." Okay. So as an adult, I hired an accountant, who I email, quickly.

Once again, it is amazing how many things in my life I have been told were "only a joke." It is even more amazing how many of them weren't funny.

When Clarence dropped dead, and his threats were then null, I had things I finally could have said. Things that I wouldn't be killed over. I, as a fourteen-year-old country girl, didn't get this on a conscious level. That, I think, would have been far too overwhelming. I kept silent.

But that season has passed. Now I am telling you.

Dreams

When I went to work on *The Quick and the Dead,* I had just done *Basic* and was so happy to be out in the middle of the Arizona desert, so happy to be in a Western—though not a traditional Western. I loved Clint Eastwood, thought he was the ultimate cowboy. I thought that Gene Hackman was one of the greatest actors alive. I asked the studio to offer him the lead. I also asked them to give him top billing. They so didn't understand me, and wouldn't.

I wanted this guy they had never heard of for the other male lead, the Australian guy I had seen play a very dangerous skinhead in a movie called *Romper Stomper.* His name was Russell Crowe. They thought this was absurd. Why did I want a foreign actor who had played a bald psychopath to play a minister in a period piece in the Old West, someone we would have to push and wait two weeks for? Then we auditioned teens to play Gene's son, the rejected kid who just wanted his father's love. This kid named Leonardo DiCaprio was the only one who nailed the audition, in my opinion: he was the only one who came in and cried, begging his father to love him as he died in the scene. Again: "Why an unknown, Sharon, why are you always shooting yourself in the foot?" The studio said if I wanted him so much, I could pay him out of my own salary. So I did.

Next we came to the director. I wanted Sam Raimi, who at that time they thought of as a "D-movie director," as he had made the movies *The Evil Dead I* and *II* and *Army of Darkness*, which I thought were brilliant. I said he would work nearly for free as an enticement. Well, they hired him. He was very good. But when I said I wanted Danny Elfman of Oingo Boingo to do the music, they cracked and locked me out of the editing room. The consensus was that "you cannot put modern music on a Western." I can say that studio heads are not always ahead of the curve, to put it kindly. Danny Elfman has of course had a legendary career doing many films and won a Grammy for "The Batman Theme." But no woman star, and certainly not I, with my foot-shooting ideas, was going to be telling anyone what to do, whether I was a producer or not.

Getting a producer credit as an actress is often thought of in my business as a "vanity deal," meaning they pay you for the job but shut the fuck up and stay out of the way. I won't accept a vanity deal and let them know that up front. This is illegal, I say, and I like to work within the law. That gets a lot of silence and not a lot of joy on the other end.

Perhaps it is because as a producer I did things that other producers don't do. For example, when someone died on my set, I shut the show down and sat with the cast and crew until the ambulance or helicopter came for the body. Yes, we sit in silence and respect. I pull the plug for the time it takes. This is not common, but it is the way I work.

When someone is too high to work, I let the studio know. That isn't always a popular choice, but it's mine. I don't burn other people's money to be popular. For me it's called show business, not show take advantage of everyone. I don't get taken advantage of either. Yes, I have been asked or told to do things that are wildly inappropriate, but I use my big-girl voice and say no.

In the same regard, I work a lot of hours a long way from home, and some of my best relationships have started on set.

I met Bob Wagner on the set of *The Quick and the Dead*. He was the second assistant director. He wouldn't make a pass at me, maybe, probably, as I was the star and it would have been bad form and Bob is just too elegant for that. So I made a pass at Bob. He went for it and we were together for quite a while.

He was, for much of my life, the love of my life. We were movie lovers; more, we were film-obsessed. I loved to cook dinner and eat it in bed with Bob while we watched Criterion films. We were students of film—we would argue and laugh and talk about film. He showed me his favorites and I showed him mine and we watched every film we hadn't seen.

We left *The Quick and the Dead* and went on to *Casino*. I had asked for him to be hired too. I didn't want to face the Scorsese–De Niro–Pesci group all by myself. Thank God he got to go. I never could have done it without him. I never would have been nominated for the Oscar without him. In a business, a town where no one seemed to care or respect a woman doing her best, to have a boyfriend who not only believed in me but helped me do it was incredible. It never would have happened without that support. It meant everything to me.

Roy London did not live to see me do *Casino* or to help me understand what to do when I held my dream in my hand. The first time I went to his little apartment before we both became so famous and successful, he asked me what my goal was. I said, "I want to be good enough to sit down opposite Robert De Niro and hold my own."

There is a scene in *Casino* where I have gone astray from my husband, played by Mr. De Niro. I walk into a restaurant and sit down. I have very little dialogue; the scene is essentially his. But in that scene, I hold my own. It is the scene I do for Roy. I have held what became our dream.

When that movie was over I was so exhausted; I gave every piece of myself to that character, to that goal. Martin Scorsese was the greatest director of my life. He worked with me so deeply and guided me so gracefully. Mr. De Niro taught me more by the example of his incredible work ethic than any other actor I have ever seen work in my forty years in the business. He works into a character as if fitting on a second skin. He will not stop until it is a perfect fit: no matter how long or how difficult or how many takes or how complex the emotional contortion. He is the master. I did my best to be his partner, stride for stride. When the movie began, he told me that his performance depended on mine. I took him seriously and did everything I possibly could not to let him down.

Thank goodness that my life has led me to meet and talk with Mick Jagger, who gave me a great on-the-road tip. He told me that in order to get any decent sleep, when he got to a new town, he bought multiple rolls of aluminum foil and masking tape and then put the foil all over the windows in the hotel bedrooms. I did this as we went into night shooting. My room was a tomb. I would come in and fall onto the bed fully clothed, and my cat, Boxer, would wrap himself around my head, digging his claws into me, padding me until I fell asleep.

Bob Wagner took the most amazing care of me. We worked endless hours. We could get the casinos only if the "whales" weren't in there gambling. If they came in, we were done. Sometimes we had a good six hours of work and sometimes a good twenty-three. Crew members had car accidents falling asleep at the wheel.

But Bob, oh, Bob: I overran the bathtub over twice to the point that it was a waterfall into the bedroom. Bob said, "I got this, honey, don't you worry about a thing, you are going to the show, just keep doing what you are doing, I've got you," and he did. I had an ovarian crisis midproduction, needing to go to the hospital for a week for endometrial surgery. I stayed on the night schedule, as we all were night-shooting. Marty kept talking to me at night on the phone from work so I could stay awake and sleep in the day. Bob took care of me and continued to work those hideous hours.

We left that show and he went to work on a show with Jodie Foster directing. I went with him and stayed in my pajamas the whole time. I just put a coat over my jammies and went to lunch or wherever trying to recover from being Ginger. All of the time my fame was growing and crushing his spirit. He was doing everything for me and for us and my life was a rocket. He used to wish I were a diner waitress. I once had been. And now this.

We eventually broke up when it all got to be too damn much. My health was failing. I was told if I was going to have a baby it was then or never. Bob wasn't ready—he was nine years younger than I. It was killing us. For two decades we tried to just love each other in separate universes and sometimes the same one.

I made bad choices; I tried to move on.

Eventually I had to place this love somewhere; I have, he has. I probably made more of it than he did. I'm like that. But I can say that the day I was nominated for the Oscar for *Casino*, when one line rang and I thought, *Oh, I didn't make it,* and then all of the home and office lines rang at the same time and I thought, *Oh, holy cow, it happened!!!!!* and then the gate line rang and I knew it was Bob with Champagne: that was the line I answered.

Dancing Lessons

Kelly's friends from childhood often stayed family friends for life. On 9/11, two of them—Robin and Dawn, who had become like sisters—were on vacation with us on Nantucket Island.

On 9/10, we had been at a karaoke bar all night after golfing all day. I am not much of a karaoker, and not a drinker, so when we got back to the old house we had rented, I stayed up to watch the morning news and was sitting there watching when the second plane hit the tower.

I immediately called to rent a truck at Boston Harbor to be there waiting for us, and started trying to figure out how to get us to the mainland. Finally I sat there collecting my thoughts before putting on the coffee and waking the "kids," which is what Kelly, Robin, and Dawn had suddenly become to me again.

Time evaporated, and I was the big sister who needed to get it together. Grateful that I had been taught not to fall down on the job.

We ended up getting on the last ferry leaving Nantucket

before travel was shut down. It was for me an unnerving crossing. I drove us to my parents' place in Pennsylvania, where I thought we would all be safe. We were.

I left Robin and Dawn in Penna, where they lived at the time, and Kelly and I began to drive west. We drove for a couple of days before the airports opened again. We left the truck and flew home, having become even closer.

I arrived back in the Bay Area in time to throw out the opening pitch for an Oakland A's game, which I had been previously booked to do. The Athletics had asked for my favorite number for my jersey. As I jogged out toward the mound with the number 11 on my back, helicopters overhead and snipers strategically placed throughout the stadium, I realized how much the crowd wanted, perhaps *needed*, me to make it to the plate.

I could have moved in to throw it. I thought about it—who wants to fail? But years earlier, Tommy Lasorda, then the Dodgers' manager, had helped me when I needed to learn to pitch for a TV show I was doing. He took my call and set me up with a guy from the team to teach me; he didn't blow me off or make fun of me. That day, he was on my shoulder. I made it to the plate: barely, but still I got it there.

All too soon, my own collapse would come, and I would find myself lying on the TV room floor, feeling like I had been shot in the head, wondering where that someone was who would protect me, who would keep me safe.

Weeks later, after a seven-hour brain surgery, where my ruptured right vertebral artery was replaced by coils in a complicated attempt to save my life, I woke up in intensive care with one perfect chance of surviving. When I heard about everything that had happened, I tried to rip the Dilaudid out of my vein, only to be told that I had to step down off of the drugs so as not to go into seizure. Oh, great, now I was a drug addict. No one told me my terrible odds. I read those in *People* magazine.

The nurse came to put in a new IV, and while he was rolling my shrunken vein over and over again, he proceeded to tell me about all of the roles I had taken that he found disappointing. Not only the roles themselves but my work was disappointing, and he demanded an explanation for this.

He rolled and rolled my vein. I started to think that maybe he was an assassin. I got very quiet and ever so sneakily, bit by bit, got to the call button. Finally another nurse came after what felt like an eternity. I tried to be perky. "Hey, we're having a bit of trouble with my vein—maybe someone else could have a try?" I looked at her, trying to summon up some of that on-the-spot acting to demonstrate severe desperation so she would read my mind. It seemed to work, and she ushered him out.

I was overwrought with the thoughts of what a shitty actress I was. I called a career counselor and had her come to the hospital. She sat there, purse in lap, ever so composed, looking at me as if to say, *You need to simply get well, lady.* This is a fabulous example of why we should just say no to drugs.

I was up all night and slept all day. I had nonstop dreams that I was learning some kind of code, a digital code, and that this code was being given to me by five angels. I could sleep only when the sun shone. In the darkness I was seeing the dark, seeing the fibers in the air, feeling the emptiness, listening for my son. I wasn't sure if I would live or die, and I wasn't sure if I was supposed to live or die.

I was one of the lucky few who beat the odds and walked out of the rubble of the neurological ICU. Walked out past the still-screaming eighteen-year-old in the bed next to me, trying desperately to straighten her spine—there with no parents, being taken care of by her younger sister. I walked past the empty bed across from the nurses' station, now quiet, empty of the soul who had floated upward; past the laboring machines, the exhausted nurses, their kind and noble faces still holding me upright.

I was walking, a ragged, tilted walk, my right leg dragging a bit, the left side of my face distorted and low, no feeling from the knee up in my left leg. I was talking, not knowing I was stuttering, not realizing that the walls didn't really have blocks of colors on them. I'd lost directional hearing in my right ear and so much weight. I was now a whopping size two, at five feet, eight and a half inches. As the sun hit my face outside of the hospital, I felt small, thin to my core. It was hard to stand, but standing felt so good.

If you want to survive a brain hemorrhage, or I'm guessing any major life-and-death struggle, the first thing you have to learn to do is trust. But who? I could have gold-medaled at the Olympics of Paranoia at this point. You don't get a lot of sleep when you have neurological damage, or at least not sleep when other people are sleeping. My brain was trying to rewire itself.

One day someone came to the house to give me a manicure

and pedicure. The girl spoke very little English; she was Vietnamese. I put my feet in the soothing water—it was marvelous. She picked up my foot and said something like, "Ishayotoe?" I asked her two or three times, trying to get it, I was already so hazy. Then she picked my foot up and showed it to me. I had so much hair on my feet I looked like a monkey. She looked at me again and now I clearly understood: "I shave your toes?"

So now I was Bigfoot. I was whoever made it out of neurological ICU, and, baby, that is way harder than it looks. I was calm, observant, nonreactive, I had to listen. I had to listen because my right ear was so f'ed up that I had to turn my head to the left and watch people's lips to understand what they were saying. Oh, yeah, I got it but good. I got the big spanking.

It is amazing how much one learns when one has to. I became "Miss Peace and Fucking Quiet," a title that I prize much higher than a Miss Crawford County pageant title. I went back to being a "hippie."

My parents were a rock. My mother cooked every dish from my childhood that I had long ago given up for the sake of my modeling and film careers. She was getting those pounds back on me. My father was a sentinel. I slept all day and was up all night. I felt like I was communing with the stars, the universe. I had an incomplete sense of what was going on around me. One morning the gardener came in the house and I recoiled in terror from this stranger in my kitchen. I thought he was a burglar. I was panic-stricken until I absorbed the incredible compassion on his face as he explained who he was. Then the dime dropped. I had lost my short-term memory.

Now I look back at all of it, the hideousness of all of it, the unbearable pain of recovery: how I could be sitting on the couch and it would feel like someone had punched me in the face; my head would swivel, I would make a sound as if hit, and my face, only on that side, would suddenly turn bright red. Or I would get brutal pains on the top of my head and these inch-high lumps would come up, scattered over my scalp. Or my leg would feel like it was bleeding or wet, or burning. My fuse box was so messed up it was sending all kinds of weird signals all over the place. I was about to find out that I wouldn't be able to read for another two years or remember where I'd put down my teacup. But I was up and I was alive and I had a one-and-a-half-year-old baby boy who needed a mother. I didn't know how I would do it, but I knew I would.

As I drifted through my days, sitting by the window in my bedroom looking at the ocean, mending Roan's Teletubbies or trying to locate my teacup, I felt a peacefulness that was different from anything I had personally known before. After about a week I felt well enough to try to go downstairs again. My dad took me for a walk and a sit in my garden. I took Jacqueline Kennedy Onassis's book of favorite poems, which I had just been given as a gift.

In order to hear him read them to me above the sounds of the ocean or the occasional car going by, I had to turn my left ear to him and concentrate on the movement of his lips. This would not allow me to jump ahead inside myself and form my own answers or conclusions to what he was saying. I couldn't agree or disagree in advance. I had, in fact, to learn and to listen. To really listen to what another human being was saying and then consider it and respond. My hearing had been modulated to give me the gift of truly listening and staying present.

We opened the book. I started to browse through it, looking for a poem, perhaps one that the fabulous Mrs. O. and I both knew and loved, when I started to see spots on the page. I thought I was just tired. Maybe too much for one day. My dad and I talked some more. I had never realized quite how interesting he was: how tender and funny he could be and what good company. He helped me back to my room. I was exhausted.

As I came to recognize that I had lost not only some of my short-term memory but some of my long-term memories too, I wondered what that might mean. Which memories and why? Which things was my brain kicking out in an effort to survive? While this was interesting, I also wondered if in fact I had died that day and was now a new person, a new me. I wondered if I was in a sense starting over.

So I made a commitment to truth. To stop putting sensationalistic crap in my head. It cut down on the confusion. In order to do this, I could tell only the truth as well. I spent hours by the window considering if I could do that differently. I had been cruel with the truth. Perhaps I could just be quiet and allow. There is a lot of strength in allowing, and I was so weak. Allowing others their truth. Allowing things to unfold. Allowing things to reveal themselves so that everyone could see for themselves. Allowing spirit to arrive in whatever forms it comes to each individual to bring peace. Sometimes being quiet lets the truth come more loudly. I didn't know that this could be very dangerous too.

I stopped responding to argumentative situations. I found

myself observing others and myself. I loved watching Fred Rogers and *Mister Rogers' Neighborhood* and I was quite amazed to recognize how similar his principles are to the principles of Buddha. Simplicity and kindness, purity of heart and spiritual elegance, seemed to flow together as a common thread wherever I allowed myself to see this unfolding. Since I was simply unable to respond to anything quickly, I learned that there was time to choose and choose better if I could respond more thoughtfully.

Of course this caused tension, as people wanted the me I had left behind. I started to consider that the shedding of that me, however painful and dangerous, and however lauded she may have been, could be a victorious event. This newly risen incarnation might not be as fast, glamorous, or thrilling, but I had a feeling she had legs—even if they were a little wobbly at that moment, even if they would never be as beautiful again.

I wasn't sure if my whole life as I had known it would be left behind. Some of my true friends were there and steadfast, but some found the whole thing far too overwhelming and disappointing. I didn't know if I would ever be well enough to work again: to remember my lines, look presentable, and be photographed as Sharon Stone. I'd lost my place in line. I didn't know if living at all was an accomplishable task, given my state of affairs.

I lay awake at night asking myself how to go on. I couldn't see normally: I was seeing colors on the wall and the floor undulating below me as I walked; every time I blinked there were lightning-like flashes at the corners of my eyes. When I tried to discuss this with my doctors, they would do routine tests on me. I would touch my nose with my eyes closed, stand on one leg, jump on one leg, get my knee whacked with a small hammer, and be told, "You are doing just fine." I had survived, and given what I had endured, that in itself was so rare that, to everyone else, all of the rest of it was dismissible.

No one recommended any kind of aftercare for me. So for months I lived in this abyss. Lost, wondering, sleeping, devastated. Then one day my small son came into my bedroom and with all of his might pushed over the set of tools by the fireplace. This made the most incredible crashing sound. My head felt like it would burst. I couldn't believe it. I looked at him standing there in his tiny one-piece outfit and he looked up at me in bed and said, "No more jammies, Mommy." He was fighting for me. He had made a stand.

I honestly didn't know what to do. I loved him so much and I knew he needed me and I needed him. The distance from the bed to the floor was so far. I'd been out of context for months. I loved him so much.

I pulled myself out of bed, took a bath with him sitting by my side. I got dressed. I made an effort. I called my friend Quincy Jones in L.A., who I knew had had two aneurysms and not only survived but was a top man in his profession and a great humanitarian. He took me under his loving, generous wing. He invited us to Christmas dinner.

When we arrived at his house a few weeks later, he took one look at me and said, "You are not okay."

"No," I said. "I can't see. I'm scared. I don't know what to do."

"I want you to see the very best doctor. He will take care of you," he reassured me in his loving way. Of course the doctor, Hart Cohen, was away for the holidays, but I spoke to him on the phone, and even on the phone he was very easily able to tell me that I had a brain-seizure condition that could be treated with one of seven medications, and he made an appointment to see me. I was hopeful but not convinced.

But I saw him. I started one of the medications. It did help but was not perfect for me; I rapidly gained a lot of weight and my symptoms did not completely abate. Of course my appearance in L.A. caused attention: Oscar season was approaching, and the next thing I knew I had been asked to present an Oscar with John Travolta. I went back to the doctor in tears.

He took a look at me and, with his soft-spoken assuredness, said, "You are going to do it. No problem—you'll see." He put me on a new medication and a special diet of high-protein foods. I never deviated. I had a goal. In a matter of days I could see. The flashes stopped, the colors stopped, my speech difficulties abated, and my hearing was gradually improving. Within a couple of weeks I went to the Oscars rehearsal. I tried to fit in. I was introverted, like someone who had been in deprivation therapy. Everyone was very busy being fabulous, and I was working hard to stand. It was an interesting perspective. I had a lot of compassion in a way that I just had not imagined before. I saw my fellow artists as artists, fragile and covered in social masks in order to cope with the pressure of these huge expectations. I was still, gentle, and apart. I found unobtrusive ways to be in this chaotic environment, feeling sage, not needy or nervous, understanding how much effort was being put out. I could see how hard everyone else was working to be liked.

Of course John Travolta, who I was so lucky to have been coupled with, has a remarkable gift of dance. Just to see him can make a person light up and want to smile and dance. I mean, those photos of him dancing with Princess Diana are legendary.

I mentioned that it might be fun to dance onto the stage. Of course I didn't know if I was really able to dance, but I wanted to push myself toward a bigger goal; after all, I was walking now. He didn't respond at first. I let it go. The next night, when we arrived for the actual Oscars, I was sitting in the hallway on a steamer trunk as he walked by. He asked to see my dress. I shyly stood up as he twirled me around.

"Good dancing dress," he said in his famously charming way. "Let's do it. Let's come out from opposite sides and dance down the stage."

My heart was racing. Just two weeks before, I had struggled with walking. Now I would be dancing. I could do this. I could dance. I looked into his eyes. I said yes. He walked away. I said a prayer to the universe: "Let me do it for me. Let me do it for everyone who needs to know they can."

I stepped into my joy, my gratitude; I had made it this far. Faith is the question. Faith is the answer. Believe. This had become my mantra. I floated down that stage and looked into the faces of all of my talented, amazing fellow Academy members. They were smiling, laughing, and digging the moment. All of us uplifted. They didn't need to know why.

Answered Prayers

There is not much that is more painful or more toxic to the body than its own blood where it doesn't belong. Or so they told me when I continued to wonder why the hell my life still felt like ragged pieces of dirty Kleenex. It took about two years for my body to absorb all of the blood that had blown into it.

I thought I should exercise but I was afraid if I walked quickly, my heart would beat too fast and I would have another stroke (probably in front of the neighbors' house, the ones who wouldn't wave back) and die on the sidewalk. I thought I should work. But still I couldn't see well enough to read. It turns out that although I had had LASIK eye surgery just a few months before the brain bleed and could see like an eagle or a hawk or whatever bird it is that can really see, after this thing happened, suddenly I just could no longer see correctly: elongated words, smeared words, dark areas, discoloration. I went to a neurological eye doctor, Howard Krauss. I had met so very many doctors that I felt like a medical expert. I learned that glasses would not help. I had brain damage. Could be funny, a punch line: tall blonde with big boobs and long legs has brain damage. Funny. Two years, Dr. Krauss said. Two years and we'll see. It will probably clear up. It did. Then I was middle-aged and needed reading glasses. I am a punch line. Or a punched line.

So I got a new agent, who told me I was off of the approval lists at the studios. I hadn't had any hits in too long. I needed to be in a blockbuster. I needed to be in some moneymaking movies so I could get back in the business. Except no one really wanted to hire me because I had been out of the business. Catch-22. Another punch line.

The upside is that the first fired doctor who had jumped the gun and released the story to *People* had said that I had just had a little aneurysm that had bled out and clotted off. So no one was concerned that I was a health risk. At least I didn't have the cooties issue to contend with as well. Here in Hollywood, we are the beautiful people, after all. Those sad *People* magazine covers don't help us get work, unless they are about being single again. As we've learned, fuckable is hirable.

I never gained the weight back. I became some kind of angular, skinny version of my former self.

I don't miss her; it's like she is a person I knew very intimately, but not me. I remember my childhood, I remember the majority of my life, like every person in their sixties. But my feelings are objective about before.

I imagine that most people who survive extreme life-and-death circumstances feel this way. I speak with soldiers easily about this. I spoke to Aron Ralston, the guy who had to cut his own arm off to get out from under a boulder in a remote part of Utah. Each time I meet someone who has been to the edge, it's like we have a shorthand. There is an absence of baggage. There is a need to serve.

Over the years many people have asked me what inspired me to begin working with HIV/AIDS. I have given a lot of answers and many of them were components in the decision, but none of them were the whole truth, the actual thing that began it all in my heart and mind.

Yes, it is true, that in 1986, I came back from Africa with my first husband, Michael Greenburg, and we moved to Mandeville Canyon, where Elizabeth Glaser was our neighbor. While she was fighting to stay alive after she got AIDS from a blood transfusion, and trying to make sure her family would be safe, we helped her begin her work with the local pediatric AIDS fair on our street, which I still work on with my pediatrician, Dr. Peter Waldstein, and his wonderful wife, Laurie. Yes, it is also true that my beloved Roy London did eventually die of HIV/ AIDS, and yes, it is true that many of my friends, colleagues, and acquaintances from the modeling, art, and film worlds died of this horrible disease. But that is not the original thing.

The original thing happened when I was twenty-four and newly married to Michael, who I met while filming a television movie in Las Vegas. It was great: we were working with Rock Hudson and James Earl Jones. Not your average TV cast at that time. But then I was pawned out by my then-agent to go to work in South Africa for a company that was buying rands for dollars cheaply and thus making films for next to nothing. Richard Chamberlain and I were sent off to make the inglorious *King Solomon's Mines*. This, we were told, would take three to four months, which is what films used to take to make. *Okay, I thought. I'm a kid from the sticks—this will be like camping.* What did I know of life in the third world?

Filming actually started in Zimbabwe. When I got there and saw the conditions of the hotel, I was horrified. The carpeted floors had never been vacuumed. The hotel didn't own a vacuum cleaner; they cleaned those carpets with rags and something that smelled like ammonia. On their hands and knees, I might add, and with not-so-clean rags. The bedding was soiled with bloodstains, holes, and God only knows what else. The towels were in similar shape. This was Zimbabwe in 1984.

The first night I heard a strange sound outside of our window. Tentatively, I looked out and saw huge animals, the size of the only elephants I had ever seen (in the circus), but they weren't elephants. These animals were grazing Cape buffalo, just outside my room. I couldn't believe my eyes, they were so gigantic. Nothing like what you imagine when you see the back of a nickel. There were three of them, just looking through the window right at me. I got Michael out of bed. We stood there like two schoolkids with our mouths agape, laughing and staring at each other in wonder.

My dad had taught me how to walk in the woods silently; he had taught me all about deer and foxes, rabbits and bears—but this? Well, as it turns out, tracking is tracking. Every day after work I would lead safaris through the bush with my driver, who was simply astounded by my ability to spot and sneak up on elephants, giraffes, bat-eared foxes, hippos bathing down at the river, and all sorts of game. This became my refuge.

Michael and I decided to live on our per diem. This was the money we got for daily living expenses, such as food, laundry services, and so forth. We sent our actual salaries home to the bank. Everything we needed or wanted we laid away or waited to buy so that we lived more like everyone else around us. We wanted to live where we were, we thought.

Of course, when we first arrived, we were so naïve. We didn't realize that we had landed in the middle of a famine, a drought, locked borders, starvation, and very much the center of a crisis. At first we were sheltered by our film family, driven to work and back to the hotel.

Then the drought ended and it began to rain. At first, we got up every day and got made up and ready so that the film insurance company would acknowledge—and pay for—our attempts to work. But it was impossible to work. The rain continued for months. It was unbelievably depressing. Michael and I were vegetarians and athletes, clean-cut kids. Finally, my hairdresser brought me some black hash from the Congo. It came in a round ball, the size of a tangerine. He said, "Shazza, honey, you have to stop crying—smoke some of this and it will make you feel better." We tried it and we laughed for three days. It did make us feel better, I have to say.

The rain destroyed all of our sets, which had been built outside. We had to shut down the show. The Zimbabweans decided that Richard Chamberlain and I had brought the rain and named us the Rain King and Queen; they held a ceremony and gave us crowns of flowers and vines. The producers decided to cut their losses and make two movies instead of one.

We ended up being in Africa for a year and change. Michael went to work as a line producer for the films. He was already a television producer, so they were lucky to have him there. He went back and forth between there and the company's office in London, but I stayed.

We all became quite close in our little groups. We went through so much. There was the issue of the borders being closed, so when we lost a dolly wheel for the camera cart, we couldn't get another one. Frankly, we couldn't get anything: not decent food, nothing. I got an old television and a VCR and a huge box of tapes sent over. The first film I played was *Lawrence of Arabia*. All of the hotel staff were absolutely mesmerized when I put it on. They had never seen a film of any kind. It was wonderful.

I went to the kitchen and found flour and water and old, awful, faded-to-white canned vegetables and made some haphazard pizza. To this day, this remains the best party I ever had: black hash from the Congo, very bad pizza, and this film playing while people looked behind the TV to see where it came from. We were so happy, and it was so beautiful. We were filthy and poor and starving and full of love.

We had a Halloween party and introduced this crazy idea to everyone. I did makeovers on the ladies. The women taught me to dance. Oh my God, that was so fantastic—I finally moved my flat white ass! Those women could *really* dance. I made friends with a fabulous family there who used to be rich before the war and had an amazing broken-down old mansion and an old Rolls-Royce. Their daughter would have me over for tea and biscuits, a daily ritual that continued onto set. She would give me facials out by the chicken coop, and her mom, Maureen, would make us something to eat. They practically adopted me, and we are friends to this day.

Maureen's son, now grown, is deeply involved in saving the rhinos. He is also a wonderful musician, and it gives me so much joy that we can correspond via email now.

We used to say, "You'll love Africa—it gets in your blood, those beautiful sunsets and sunrises can't compare to anywhere. But you can never like Africa—it is too damn harsh."

It got so harsh. This really hit home for me when I started to hemorrhage and had to go to the hospital. The nurses thought I was miscarrying, and, well, I could have been. I was put on a gurney in the hall and left there. There were no meds, nothing to stop or sop up the bleeding, no doctors with time for me. There were too many tragically dying men, women, and children: on gurneys, on the floor, in all of the rooms, streaming in through the doors.

What the hell was happening? They were so sick, so terribly sick, writhing in agony, suffering, screaming out in pain. Michael brought me a couple of Valiums he had brought with him; that knocked me out, and a nurse who wiped my forehead sometimes gave me rags for the bleeding until it finally stopped, so I went back to the hotel—thank God without meds or a transfusion. I was lucky.

We left Zimbabwe and went to South Africa. It was the middle of the apartheid conflict. There were little children being machine-gunned to death just a few miles from where we were filming. Shot dead in their school chairs for no reason. People were being "tired": the act of having a tire placed around them and covered in gasoline and set on fire.

I was there when Soweto was on fire. We stole walkie-talkies from the set and organized a raid. We cut holes in the fence and got people out. We lied and broke into the production office to figure out how to make calls. We did anything we could do. I got people to give their per diems to help rebuild homes for those whose huts had been burned to the ground for voting for the "wrong" party. I gathered these funds in old coffee cans. We tweaked the satellite system so we could use the international phone lines. We tried to get help. We tried to tell people what was going on.

I helped my friend who worked on the show with us get herself and her family out of South Africa. We made it home. When we did, I found out my friend and mentor Rock Hudson was dying of HIV/AIDS. It wasn't long after that I realized *that* was what had been happening in the hospital where I was in Zimbabwe. That is what I had witnessed.

I never told anyone what I had seen. I couldn't. It was so brutal, so terrible, so beyond anything that anyone could comprehend.

Years later, when the people from amfAR, the Foundation for AIDS Research, approached me to take over for one night for Elizabeth Taylor at Cannes, I thought I would black out. I had seen what I had seen in Africa, seen people I loved in the United States die from this terrible disease, and I had thought I was helpless against it. That there was nothing I could do.

But there is never nothing.

The year I made *The Quick and the Dead,* I decided to stay in Tucson for Thanksgiving and work in the kitchen for the Salvation Army. No one there cared who I was, just that I served food hot and was kind. I loved stealing extra milk for the moms and tucking it into their babies' blankets. I loved waiting tables—I had gotten quite good at that in my college days and, before that, back in Meadville. I was fast and pleasant and knew my way around carrying six plates at the same time.

After quitting time, I went over to the children's HIV/AIDS nursery, which was a separate place altogether. There were a couple of nurses—nowhere near the amount of help needed. Quite a few of the infants were crying, but one was simply screaming in a complete psychotic break, and that is a different thing entirely. That is the kind of screaming that you never want to hear. A screaming somewhere between a cat and a child, and it is relentless.

I asked if I could pick up that child, if that would be okay. The nurse said, "Try anything." I held this little boy, this maybe six- or eight-month-old kid; it's so hard to tell with AIDS babies, or any kid with HIV/AIDS. I tried rocking him, holding him, singing to him, and while walking with him I encountered another kid of similar age, only she was completely mute. She just stared into space with a dead look in her eyes;

she had given in, given up. As I held the boy, I tried to stroke her little downy head, but to no response.

I asked the nurse, "Can I put them in together?"

"As I said, you can try anything."

So I did: I put the screamer in with the little, fluffy, nonresponsive duckling. He instantly stopped screaming. She looked at him with wonder and recognition. The nurses came over. We just stood there, teary-eyed. The two infants clearly saw something in each other. Their little hands touching, their little lost eyes looking into each other; they connected. They both awoke from their nightmares.

I was changed in that moment.

When I was at my lowest, I was so grateful that people came to see me in the hospital and that people prayed for me. I know that at some restaurants where I commonly ate, the waitstaff held prayer circles for me. I know that some nuns from Tibet prayed for me. People I barely knew and some I did not know at all prayed for my survival. I know for sure that those people kept me alive. I am bathed in gratitude. It is for that and for them that I live a life of service.

Cages

I had the greatest art teacher in high school, Mrs. Kluz. In the summer she took trips and she would record the sounds of where she was. Then she brought back those sounds and had us paint them. Yes! Paint the sounds. It was so exciting, to think about other places by their sounds. I remember when she brought back the sounds of the New York subway, I was hooked. What was that? What was that squeaking and thundering? What were all of those people talking about? Where were they going? What was happening, happening, happening? Little did I know that a year and a half later, I would be modeling among those sounds.

She had us do a project where the method of drawing represented the thing we drew. I drew a labyrinth of the word *unique*. She used mine to show the class what she meant. I felt special for the first time. Somehow she had set me free. She had a stroke that year. It completely paralyzed the dominant side of her body. She came back to school and learned to draw from the other side. She was young and hip and beautiful and she did not stop; she stayed her course. She was such an inspiration—then, and now.

There is a discipline in honoring thyself.

I sometimes wonder if I had my own stroke because I let myself get too far off of my natural path, too far away from my true journey in life. I wonder if the body cries out when we are not following our natural truth, when we are trying to fit that square peg into a round hole. Instead of just being me. Instead of being Sharon the artist, Sharon the mom, friend, sister, lover, daughter, neighbor, community member. All of the things that are natural and correct for me.

Over the course of my life, I have come to understand that when it comes to abuse, many people do not fully grasp that it is the abuser who looks strong, compelling, and in control. The victims of abuse can look shredded and insane, as if they are high or lying or in some way too fragile to believe or depend on. Their desperation seems off, unreliable. The abuser seems still, solid, in control. That is the person who has threatened the other person into submission. Of course they're in control.

The fact gets lost that ultimately the *abuser* is the weak person, the person broken and severely troubled, the person with a mental issue. Moreover, the unprepared victim does not know whether the abuser will actually follow through and kill them or do whatever is the next promised violation. If that violation is toward another person and not them, the fear is stronger, more deeply implied.

Even if the abuser peacocks around, the victim's response doesn't line up, so again, the victim is the one who seems off.

Even when the abuser lies and is caught, it simply seems like an explainable mistake, as the victim is too desperate or introverted to speak up.

Once you have been victimized, the possibility of recurrence is greater, as other abusers seem to be able to sniff this out. Unless you come clean, get help, tell your truth to someone who will listen, get PTSD therapy, and get that on the record. It is so important to let someone in the professional world know your situation. This can and will protect you and your loved ones. It is also very important to journal. Keep an account of what is or has happened to you on a locked computer with the dates of the abuse or a calendar that is locked up somewhere unavailable to your abuser. This is a legal document. It will be your best friend in the future, your advocate when you need it. This can save your life.

If it has to be, let this be the one lesson you take away from my life and experiences.

When I was researching my part for *Last Dance,* I went to the Tennessee Prison for Women, to be locked down in maximum security for one day. I had never been in a women's prison, never spoken to a maximum-security prisoner. I was to play a woman who had committed murder when she was eighteen, had been tried as an adult, and was spending her life in prison. I had reached out to the prison, and had been corresponding with a prisoner who I would meet after I spent the day in lockdown.

This meant I arrived and was completely searched—cavities

checked: nose, ears, vagina, anus—stripped of all things, including my dignity, leg-ironed, handcuffed, and led through the prison to my cell on death row. The warden assured me that my identity had not been leaked. But as I made my way through the prison, the long walk was made longer by the banging on the bars and the screams of "Fuck you, Sharon Stone, fuck you, motherfucker, fuckingsharonstonemotherfucker," and all imagined variations of this. My leg irons began cutting their first bruises into the backs of my ankles.

The small death-row pod had about nine cells. When I arrived, I learned a few things quickly. For example, the trapdoors where you put your arms out to get the cuffs removed is also how you communicate with other inmates. Consequently, "Shut your trap" takes on an immediate new meaning. When you go for a shower, it's arms out to get your cuffs, and once inside the shower, arms out to get them off—no walking anywhere uncuffed or without leg irons. The other women are not in any way happy for new company. The f-yous continued, as I used the metal pot with no seat, rested on the metal bed not tall enough to sit on without banging my head on the unused bunk above, glanced toward the window way too filthy to see any sunshine through. The room too small to walk in a circle or frankly even a straight line in. It was cold, too cold for the one rough blanket on the thin mattress to suspend the chill. But this was death row, not a Four Seasons.

At the end of my death-row day, the guards took me—still cuffed up and in leg irons, still in my orange jumpsuit—back down to meet the woman I'd been corresponding with. I met her in a sterile room with a linoleum floor and a matching table with a couple of chairs. She was a tiny blond woman, clearly once a beauty and still an intellectual. A representative from the prison stayed with us. We talked about prison life, her roommate, their relationship, what they did to handle the long days. How friendships form inside and how relationships outside fall away.

I asked her why she was inside. Like a lot of women in prison, and certainly most women on death row, she had killed her spouse. I asked her why, but she didn't want to say—she had never said. She had gone to trial, been sentenced, and had never said. Her lawyer had let it go at that. She had been the head nurse at a hospital, her husband the head doctor, and she had, by all accounts, just killed him one night when he came home for "no apparent reason." Hmmmmmm. As we ladies all know, that don't fly.

To play this part I felt I *needed* to understand, and beyond that, I felt one person should know why she let her children, all boys, live without a parent.

Well, it seems her husband had been pushing broken bottles up her vagina in a sexual act of his determination. He had been doing this repeatedly, and she snapped. She didn't want her sons to know that her husband was this man, nor that this had happened to her. She took the death penalty instead of telling anyone or shaming her family with this terrible story.

I so understood this, more as my own life went on—not wanting to tell anyone the terrible things men had done to me, though nothing as terrible as this. They were private and privately held, and I understood not wanting anyone, or even and especially your children, to know the world their mother had lived or was living in. I took it too, held it inside, never told.

I thanked her. For many years after, I encouraged her and her prison counselor to get her new legal representation and get her a retrial, but there has been no movement.

Women stay in contact with one another psychically, energetically. We tell one another things by a thought. Some people call it women's intuition, but whatever you call it, we have it. And this woman will be forever in my thoughts.

When I filmed the scene in *Last Dance* where my character gets a reprieve and steps off of the killing table during her execution, all of this blew out of me like a gale force. I crumbled and fell apart. No one at work wondered what was going on. In fact, my loyal and deeply empathetic crew waived their overtime and finished the rest of the scene where the reprieve is overturned, and my character is killed, and we worked long hours until dawn. We all put our own emotions out onto that killing machine and our own thoughts about it into that scene. We did that terrible journey together, and I am ever grateful to them for their deep professionalism and tremendous empathy.

Bob went with me on this film too, and took care of me again. And that night he sat, all night, at the bar down the street, unable to come in and watch this thing happen to me, but holding a space of security and safety.

I was lucky to be working with Bruce Beresford—known for such films as *Driving Miss Daisy*, *Breaker Morant*, *Tender Mercies*, and *Crimes of the Heart*—as he is not one of those directors who say, "That was great—can we do another take?" No, he says either "That was the one—moving on" or "That was just awful—do anything else, *anything* but that," which makes me laugh and sets me free. I adore him and his kooky ways, and he kept me right on the tips of my toes.

As we approached the end of the shoot, after three months of working in a brand-new, as-yet-uninhabited prison, the crew chef asked me what I wanted for my last meal. I said Thanksgiving dinner. He made it with all of the trimmings: turkey, mashed taters, cranberry sauce, pie, the whole thing. We all loved it, and it brought such nostalgia. There is so much love on location: the driving in with the trucks, the unloading—it's like a circus coming to town, the way the departments do their jobs and the way we make something out of nothing.

I just love my crews; I walk around watching them do their magic and I am amazed. Just amazed. The instant transformation from nothing to everything: no one but movie crews can do that. Sure, we live like gypsies, live all day in motor homes, or stand around in blistering heat or freezing cold, eat off paper plates and out of steam trays, and bitch about all of it. However, we will all take care of one another completely. There is a strange loyalty, a knowing of what we are.

I often think moviemaking is like the army for hippies. We must arrive on time and that time is not nine-to-five. It's more like 7:13 or 5:06. Our times are precise and emphatically meant. We break at exact times and come back exactly. We stay in our own departments. We follow a lot of rules. We must be ready, on time, and prepared. There is zero time for those who can't keep it together. Time is money, and a lot of it. We cannot afford to lose ten or twenty minutes because someone can't do their part. We earn our respect.

When we have to go to the bathroom, we have to tell someone, normally an assistant director, and it has to be approved so we don't screw everyone up. It's called a ten-one-hundred and it's not private. It goes out over a walkie-talkie, "Sharon is ten-one-hundred." Obviously, no one goes to the bathroom and hangs out on the phone. Lunch is thirty minutes, to eat, use the bathroom, brush your teeth, and get back to hair and makeup for touch-ups if you are in the acting department. This has caused a bad habit of eating standing over the sink. This is if you get lunch. I was on a show recently that paid the lunch penalty and we worked twelve to fourteen hours with no break at all.

Also, for the ten years of the on-fire piece of my career this caused me to skip all medical needs. Dislocated shoulder: suck it up. Root canal in my trailer with no novocaine at lunchtime: that was not a great one, I can say; I had that redone twice— and then had total jaw surgery to repair the damage from this absolutely stupid behavior. Bursting ovarian cyst: get some super-strong meds, and change it from a standing scene to a sitting scene. Broken foot from an overzealous stuntman: get a bigger boot for that foot, finish the show, and then get it rebroken and repaired after the show wraps. In other words, shut up and deal. There isn't room for babies in this biz, especially if I, as a woman, want to prove my mettle.

When I stopped working so much in the late nineties and

started to repair my war wounds, some people couldn't believe that I really did need a pin in my shoulder and 250 stitches— from being hit by an uninsured motorist, driving the wrong way up Sunset Boulevard when I was coming home from acting class—as the sports medicine doctor insisted, or my four-month-old baby was going to pull my arm right out of the socket. Yes, I really did need to get my teeth repaired at long last. Yes, my ovaries had seen way too much. It seems your periods do stop when you overwork, undereat, and stress yourself to the limit making movies and then fly night and day to sell them.

After I had the operation to remove the tumors in my breasts—the operation that would later come to cause so much trouble for the folks in the neurological ICU—I needed reconstructive surgery. Remarks were made about my "plastic surgery issues." This, in fact, was my issue: I went to get reconstructive surgery, assuming I would wake up looking exactly as I had before this process. Instead, my plastic surgeon thought that I would look better with bigger, "better" boobs. I left there bandaged, and when unbandaged, discovered that I had a full cup-size bigger breasts, ones that he said "go better with your hip size—I'm certain you look better now." He, in all of his self-determined knowledge, had changed my body without my knowledge or consent. I was humiliated when I went to the underwear department and stood there looking for the most sympathetic-looking woman to tell her I didn't know how to buy a bra and I didn't know what size I wore and I didn't know how to do this thing. And I still frankly don't. I also don't know if I should be angry at the now-dead plastic surgeon, whether I should get more reconstructive surgery to look like myself, or whether I should simply be happy I don't have cancer.

When I say to the press that I have my original breasts, what I mean is that I have my skin, my nipples, and my health.

But still, at some point in all of this, I lost track of myself. All of the self that I had worked so hard to build. The self-educated woman, the individual thinker, the worldly philanthropist, the movie star, the good friend, the devoted client, the respected professional, the consistent daughter, the good sister, the world traveler—and on and on. It all melted away.

I had loved walking with my baby to the pipe organ concerts they held every weekend at the museum near where we lived. I loved taking him to the movies in his little car seat. He loved musicals, then going for an ice-cream cone, smearing it all over his face. It was gorgeous. I loved showing off my son. My beautiful son. My Roan.

I loved everything about him. His smell, his little bald head sprouting white hair, those giant blue eyes. His fat feet, which were very smelly. I called him "Stinky Cheese Feet." He loved that.

And then everything went to shit.

I'd tell you what, but I signed a confidentiality agreement and I can't. And I respect my child, and I won't. But I'll tell you this: I was punished for changing the rules of how we see women, and I understand that by writing this book I could be punished again. But this time I'm not afraid.

After I lost primary custody of Roan, I couldn't function. I just lay on the couch. I was so damn tired. I slept every afternoon; I just couldn't get up. Then my dear friend and Roan's godmother got diagnosed with breast cancer and she found out she had the BRCA gene. She was also a single parent. We, all of her closest friends, decided we had better go get our mammograms. While I was there, my doctor noticed that I had a skip in my heartbeat and also suggested I do a treadmill test. There I had some kind of cardiac flip-out, so they put me on a table and called in a group of doctors. It seemed I might need a pacemaker.

Well, I considered that I would need to go somewhere private to find out. I certainly didn't need more publicity at this point—it could provide yet another reason to cut back my already-diminished custodial rights, as clearly this lapse in my health had already worked against me. I went to the Mayo Clinic. Yep, I had a prolapsed valve, but guess what? I was also anorexic. Yessiree, I had stopped eating and fallen apart and hadn't even noticed. I had just lain down and given up. My heart, it seemed, was actually broken. I had an extra beat in the upper and lower chambers of it. My Buddhist teacher, Tenzin, said my heart was expanding to accept this part of my destiny.

My friend Richard Gere once described a meditation: "Gone, gone, gone. Gone, gone, completely gone. Enlightenment." It seems obvious until it actually goes, goes, goes.

The head of the clinic said they could give me antidepressants and the name of a good psychiatrist or a book on how to eat correctly so that I could take a year or two off and exercise, eat right, and figure out my life. I chose to do that. I closed my office, ate right, and figured myself out.

I was at my dentist getting my teeth cleaned, which I have to do every four months, as the brain medicine makes my teeth weak and causes plaque buildup. I know—too much information, but where is that line now? The dentist was telling me about her weekend, which she and her office manager had spent at a women's prison. "Giving dental care?" I asked, thinking how brave and cool that was. No: she told me she had been there teaching those women how to forgive themselves. I was blown away. She was teaching convicted felons how to forgive themselves. This hit home.

I asked her if they could teach me the same. She was confused. I wanted them to come to my house and teach me how to forgive myself for losing my son, I explained. I couldn't live with it. I was so worried that he had already lost his birth mother, and concerned that it would be damaging to lose his adoptive mom too. What could that mean in the long term for him?

They came, I learned. I forgave myself. Only God is perfect, I learned. Only God knows why. Had I done the best I knew how at the time? I had. Had I genuinely tried my best? Yes. Had I loved him all of the time with all of my heart? I knew that I had. Why was I mad at a little boy? Because I missed him so much.

I made a Buddhist altar about my son. I put his picture there. I wrote notes to him and put them in my prayer bowl and meditated so that I withheld nothing and released my emotions in a healthy way.

In the meantime I met Amma, the Hugging Saint. I knew

about her, had read about her and seen her on TV, but had never seen her in person. She goes around the world hugging people and offering them blessings. That's it. That's what she does. She gives so much comfort to so many. This is a tremendous and exhausting effort of generosity and compassion.

When you go to see her, which generally happens in the biggest spaces in the biggest hotels, it's set up so you can sit and meditate and hear the live music that is playing, and then get in line when you are ready to go and receive this blessed hug. Volunteers direct you to approach her in your stocking feet, kneel down with your child or your family or your friends, and bend into her lap as she embraces you, hugs you, so deeply and warmly, holds you there, blesses you as you take in what it truly feels like to receive unconditional love, the love of a clear, pure heart. Many people bring her offerings of flowers or fruit from their gardens and she in turn responds with chocolate kisses for the children and apples for the mothers.

When, in 2007, she was given the Prix Cinéma Vérité, an award given by a French film organization focused on creating awareness of human rights issues, I was invited to speak at the ceremony. I was humbled and honored and thrilled, as I would not only meet her but, I hoped, get one of her famous hugs. I wanted to be hugged like that. I was: it was like being hugged by a cloud, a warm cloud that smelled like goodness and felt like love. She talked to me in her native Indian tongue. She believes that it is her duty to bring comfort to those who suffer, a duty she took on in her childhood. We became instant friends.

Now she is one of my dearest compatriots. Every time we are

in the same city, I go and sit with her while she hugs. Well, first I get a hug. She whispers, "Daughter, daughter, daughter," in my ear and hugs me while I cry, a little bit with joy. And now I understand that she has healed me and allowed me to become *daughter, daughter, daughter.* She allows me to sit next to her for as many hours as I care to, discussing my life, my efforts of service, my efforts of growth, and to observe her service to others. It is glorious. It is safe. It is liberating.

Amma always asks me what I am up to, what I am working on. Finally, after over half a decade of being so angry, so hurt, so without cause, and ungrounded, I answered, "I am working on forgiving the unforgivable."

"Good one!" She clapped her hands and beamed at me as if I were her star pupil. "How is it going?"

"Well, I am doing really well with the forgiving part," I answered honestly—as I was super-cool with my former marriage and the weight of child support and all that. But I couldn't get over the unending taking of my son.

"Okay, you have to put the unforgivable in a cage," Amma said.

"Like at the zoo or the circus?" I asked.

"Yes."

"Okay." I tried to imagine this. "Got it."

"Now never go to the cage."

"That's it?"

"Yes," she replied.

I sat there for a long time, maybe an hour. I had to let that sink in.

I watched her do her thing, and boy, did she.

What she helped me learn is that even compassion has boundaries. It is not for those who get up each day and choose a path of discord. This includes me.

I have learned that I do not deserve compassion either if I do the same. I participated in this discord too. It took a long time to let go. To completely stay away from the cage.

For so long I too had a crocodile smile lurking inside of me, just waiting for an excuse to come out and bite.

It took so long to get to empty. To stop. To let go. To forgive myself fully.

I forgave that little girl who didn't know what to do. That child who had been threatened with her own death, threatened by a madman. That child who was waiting for a hero, who would believe all frauds and would fall victim to herself again and again. Believing the story she had made up about how this hero looked, so that every time someone came close, someone acted, looked, or smelled like that fraudulent thing, she believed he had come, he would save her.

I went to that cage and I opened it.

I opened the door to my own cage and freed myself. My illnesses ended. I demanded good medical care and got it. I respected myself and, with compassion for my whole self, got it. I learned that my anger was a beautiful thing. A powerful part of me, like my other valuable senses, like smell and taste and touch. That anger, when used properly, when controlled, when chosen appropriately, is a valuable action.

So many people told me that it would all work out. Roan will be with you in the end, they would say.

I would cry. I would worry. I couldn't focus on anything but having my son back in my home, in my arms. Nothing else mattered. Just getting my kid back. I lost every single court battle until I didn't. I had been so sick, I had remortgaged my L.A. house, I couldn't work.

Jesus H. Christ, as my dad would say.

Fine.

I realized I had to stop resisting.

A few months later, in the summer of 2013, I was standing in my kitchen when my assistant, Tina, brought me a letter that had just come in. The first pages said that I had been nominated for the Nobel Peace Summit Award. This is the award that all of the past Nobel Peace Prize winners give each year to whoever in the world of culture and entertainment they feel has made the biggest impact in terms of promoting peace. I almost fell over while reading it.

Thankfully, Mr. Robert, my housepainter of the last thirty years, was there. He is family to me. He was eating lunch at the counter. He looked up and smiled and said, "Well, you deserve that, yes you do."

I was just getting upright when Tina said, "I don't think you read the last page." I hadn't. I looked: it said that I had won. I started to hyperventilate.

Mr. Robert just started to laugh. "See, that's what I'm talkin' about."

We went to Poland for a week for this event, and I made some lifetime friends there. It was magnificent. A huge amount of former Peace Prize winners were there. It seemed they also had to agree on who would present the award to me. Betty Williams decided that she was the only one who should do it. Betty and Mairead Corrigan had won the 1976 Nobel Peace Prize for their efforts to bring a peaceful resolution to the conflict in Northern Ireland. They did this after Betty witnessed three of Mairead's sister's children being run over by a member of the IRA, who had been shot by British troops. Mairead and Betty gathered two hundred mothers together and began to march. The next march had ten thousand mothers, the next thirty-five thousand. This activism stopped an internal war. When Betty got up and spoke about me, I met someone who already knew me. Someone who already understood me. We became a family of our own making.

She told me a story of a hired assassin who was sent to kill her. He eventually found her, and when he did, she simply talked to him. He not only spared her, he stopped killing, and is with her today working by her side, for peace. I asked her how she did that and she said, "Darlin', I loved him into submission." She is my guiding light. She is how I made it through all of this.

These days, I try to remember not to push myself harder than I can take to recover. The "no pain, no gain" theory has some very different limits for those of us who push ourselves unnaturally hard. It's more about consistency now. For me it's about the consistency of an unending journey of faith, purpose, and philosophy of living.

When I returned from the hospital, I was walking but dragging my feet. The amount of brain medicine required, and the impact of the bleed, was devastating to my system.

My life collapsed. Piece by piece I lost everything. I no longer had the ability to stand up for myself and to those whose desire, well stated, was to "break me." Break my world, they did. They broke my ego, my world as I knew it, my success as I had built it, my savings, which I had stood on four-inch heels on concrete floors sixteen-plus hours a day to earn. I was kicked when I was down.

There was no loyalty from the intimate—or perceived intimate—corner, but there was love. There was the love of my family. With crisis clearly occurring, those who had truly loved me reappeared and stood strong. There was love extended through the grapevine, and moreover there was the love that happens when people sit in prayer and thought, and that love I knew and felt deeply, and that love is what kept me alive with a 1 percent chance of survival.

His Holiness the Dalai Lama recently gave a teaching on atoms, protons, neutrons, and compassion. He said all the world is contained within an atom; there is no fear in an atom. When that idea hit me, I laughed with such incredible release, realizing my own foolhardiness each time I had tried to shove some fear in there, and the worthlessness of my efforting as I did. And I apologized to the universe for wasting its time when I knew that the time I had been given was now special and apart.

Yes, I lost many things: my career, my savings, my residential custody of my son, my so-called marriage, my place in line in regaining my career, my former ability to simply look at any page of dialogue for two minutes and have instant recall, and a kind of luminous beauty that I hadn't even realized that I'd had.

But I was no longer afraid. And without fear, I could decide to keep my integrity. I could choose to keep my soul intact. I fought a battle I knew I couldn't win in that unwelcome environment. I fought for my son, put him ahead of getting anything at all back in my life. I did that for thirteen years; I played a very long, very difficult game of custody chess in an effort to get him everything I could for his health and well-being.

Now my home and my family are complete and I am able to re-find success in the rest of my life, as my heart is also complete.

Choices

Even while all the chaos was engulfing me, I still had to live my life. I moved back to Los Angeles, and asked the adoption attorney to keep me on the list.

I was rather surprised that it worked out so quickly. Before you could say "Hallelujah," I had one more son. I felt him coming much the same as I had with Roan. Just that feeling of knowing him. I had a sense of him. The way it manifested this time is that I became obsessed with surfer movies. I watched every surfer movie I could find. My girlfriends put up with me. Some pregnant moms eat ice cream; my pregnancy by proxy was surfer movies. We loved Laird Hamilton. We went to the beach. We got new bikinis. I know this sounds nuts, but this went on for months. Finally I told Tim, who had been Roy London's life partner for ten years, "You know I am thinking of naming the baby Laird—what do you think?" and he said, "Great, honey, because that was Roy's middle name." Well, that was just the living end.

Laird was born and he wouldn't stay out of the water. He

crawled directly into the ocean when he was eight months old. Then he repeatedly threw himself into the swimming pool until my mother said, "You have got to get that kid a baby swim teacher—he's scaring the shit out of all of us." And so I did. She came to the house, got in the deep end of the pool, and told me to throw him in. I was terrified. But he went to the bottom of the pool and swam up like a dolphin and continued to swim like that for several years. He is a super athlete who at three would cannonball into the pool like he had gills. That kid loved the water so much I had to keep the garden hose locked up. He was so beautiful. He is the lover of the family. Most kids will say, "I like it," or, "I love it." Laird says, "I want to love it," before he tries anything.

Laird was three months old when I had a dream. A very vivid dream: an angel flew over me and told me that another child was coming to me. I woke up stunned and sure that this was happening. I called the adoption attorney. I asked him if he had a child for me. He said, "You just got one." I said that I was distinctly aware of that. However, I told him about my dream. He said that I was a witch and therefore he would keep an eye out.

Four days later he called me back. "I have your child."

I said, "How do you know?"

And he said, "It's the same birth parents."

I got on my knees and started to cry. I'd lost everything, my money, my career—how was I going to take care of these two kids and pay all of my legal bills with no job? I asked God, and anyone else up there who might be listening, for an ear. Then suddenly and very unexpectedly—in my forties!—I got that beauty contract with Dior. Who had ever heard of such a thing? I asked them to fly over here from Paris and take a look at me. Did they realize how old I was? They did, and they still wanted me. Someone up there had heard me.

And in short order Laird had a brother: Quinn Kelly Stone, named for my sister.

I didn't tell them, or anyone, for a long time, that they were biologically related, because it didn't feel fair. But when they were old enough to understand, I brought them to my room and told them about their special connection.

I said, "You're brothers."

They said, "We know."

I said, "No, you're really brothers; you have the same angel parents," as I had always told them that an angel princess brought them to the hospital in her tummy and gave them to me.

They turned and looked at each other as if never having really seen each other before, and in each other saw themselves.

When Laird and Quinn were little they would follow Roan around like they were in a parade. A puppy parade. They pretty much think their big brother hung the moon. Roan would gripe about them while clearly adoring them as well; it was a fabulous scene, since Roan has always had the vocabulary and the carriage of a forty-year-old, which I attribute to his adoptive father, while the younger boys behaved like little kids. Roan called Laird his assistant.

Of course bringing a new child into my space as a now-single working mom had both its complications and its joys. When I was growing up, I watched *The Andy Griffith Show* and *My*

Three Sons and the show with Sebastian Cabot as the butler and any number of shows demonstrating some idealistic look at single parenting. But single parents—and especially single mothers—are looked at by our government and by society at large as some kind of pariahs. Wealthy or poor, there must be something wrong with a person who has made this choice, seems to be the thought. Or I get a lot of *Gee, you're brave* looks. Or *How can you do it all?* questions, as though women haven't been doing it all for centuries or as though I hadn't been doing it all before, when I was still married. Let's get real. It can be a choice. A good one. A healthy, joyful, fun, exciting, interesting, hard, complicated choice.

And look at what we get. I get to be a mother. My children get to have a mother. One who is sure she wants to be one. A mother who has a job. A mother who likes her job, is proud of her work and the assets her work provides to herself and others. We get to be a family. A family who has chosen one another. We are not an accident. We are not a leaving; we are a coming together.

We have had a rather wholesome life together, simple and ordinary in our way. Dinners together and separately, cooked and ordered online. Water parks and Legoland—now outgrown. Birthday parties and sleepovers. Chubby kid legs, now a thing of the past; hand-me-downs; backpacks; stepping-up ceremonies; and lots of drawings and good papers plastering the kitchen walls and windows. All of our accomplishments on the wall. Their schoolwork next to a photo of me from a magazine. All of us just happy about our stuff.

When I was little I thought I would live in a house with a big spiral staircase in Hollywood like in a Fred Astaire/Ginger Rogers movie. I do live in a house with a big spiral staircase like in a Fred Astaire/Ginger Rogers movie, and I think that is so wonderful. What I never expected was that it would come with such a wonderful neighbor.

I first met Tony Duquette on Christmas Day. This was twenty-five years ago. It was the only Christmas I had not spent with my family in Penna ever. I had thought I would go on a trip with my best friend, but when it came down to it, I was just too spent from the rigors of becoming so famous so fast. I pretended I still might go, but just stayed home alone in L.A. I got up late, put on clean pajamas, and was making tea when my doorbell rang. My rather large, black wrought-iron gates swung open to reveal Tony, who was at that time in his late seventies, standing—well, posing—in the center in a full Swiss yodeler outfit complete with a hat with a jaunty feather, lederhosen, a green jacket, and a cane. He looked spectacular.

"Happy Christmas!" he called out. I was awestruck. He came in and looked at my place. He started up the spiral stairs in my foyer, got halfway up, and said, "Thank you for bring-ing glamour back to the film industry; Mary Pickford was my friend." Back in the day she had owned the property where my house now stood, and Tony had known her. I was simply amazed by him. He had been the set designer for all of the *Three Musketeers* films, and *The King and I,* and many fashion films. His sets and jewelry were renowned.

My house was huge and empty. All I did was work and try

to finish building it, as I had bought it unfinished. I was simply going from film to film. I came home one day, and Tony had moved lots of the set pieces and furniture from *The King and I* into my massive living room. Yes, all of those huge gold sculpture things were in my house. And that fabulous sofa! I was overwhelmed to say the least. I didn't know what I wanted, but *The King and I* set was a little too much for me. Though it was sort of super-fabulous. . . . But in my *house*?

Needless to say, I fell madly in love with Tony, who loved to smoke pot and have tea parties in his unbelievable backyard, which I can see from my balconies. A garden he made lovingly from picking up the heaps of stuff the Beverly Hills gardeners had left out for the trash over the years. In fact, his whole mansion is made of trash, of leftovers, and it is like a kingdom of glory and glamour. We used it for my home in the series *Ratched*. It was spectacular to get ready for work and go next door to Tony's to shoot. Though he is long passed now, I know he was there. Among the poppies, no doubt.

I remember being ten years old, taking a holiday meal to Betty Vozar's. She had eight or nine kids. They lived about four houses from us, which was around two miles in Pennsylvania country. She looked much like Anna Magnani, in her pale housedress and apron. There was stuff everywhere, on their stairs, on the table, on the floor, and the kids would come flying by, carrying on like a bunch of maniacs. I thought they looked so happy. Betty was always standing in the kitchen or at the kitchen table reading. While cooking.

I wanted a family like that, a house full of noise and motion. A house full of love. Learning wild love happened when I looked at my children. Sure, I had loved before. Deeply, passionately, but there is a new kind of love that happens when you love your child, at least to me. I would actually get a pain in my chest; it felt like my body might not be able to contain so much love. I might blow up.

This identity has a fuzzy-socks basket, a fire in the fireplace, dogs snoring on the couch. A library full of books to read and to look at. We are, of course, always in the kitchen. Isn't everybody? I used to just stand there when I ate the microwave dinners I had between my very important engagements.

Now I have dinners where we go around the table with the regular questions of what was the best thing and the worst thing that happened today. This made for some great dinner conversation. Lots of laughter. I think of the time when Quinn, aged five, pulled down his PJ pants and mooned all of us in the middle of dinner, his personality set in motion as the family clown. Or Roan, who could build a computer from the outside in at twelve. Laird always explaining the dearest things to us, sweet as sugar, calm and kind.

As I am raising boys as a single mom, there are delicate moments, of course. Moments when I need to take them into a room and say, "This is one of those times when I have to do Dad duty—this could be awkward, so let's both prepare ourselves." And we do, and then say when we are ready. Then we leap forward and discuss things. Obviously, these are delicate things, and things that I am unsure how to do.

I am concerned about how computer porn might affect my kids' generation, and how to talk to them about not losing the most beautiful parts of life and love, which the overwhelming greed of the world is delighted to steal. To show them false and violent things so that this sensationalism will overtake them.

Now, you are thinking: *Is this really the* Basic Instinct *woman daring to tell us this?* Yes, it is. That movie made people disassociate my humanness from me. I am the one who certainly should be telling you this. I am the one who stood by bedsides watching people die because of this.

I have an office on the property, but when the kids were little, they asked me to move my desk into the kitchen, so I did. I would be on the phone having an international conference call with both of my little kids on my lap. Everyone was just fine with it. Somehow, I think it broke people down.

Yes, they run my life. I have learned through these experiences what other parents tried to help me understand long ago: childhood goes by so quickly. I do not want to miss it. I waited until my youngest was thirteen before I took any work out of town. By choice, not by circumstance. I rarely go out at night. Even though they can babysit themselves, I want to be here.

Even though they hurt my feelings when they ignore me and when they say, "You're always here!" inside I know they want me to be there. I went over to Kelly's house two days in a row after she got an apartment near my house and they said, "Where are you going?" as if I were committing a crime. I said I was leaving for good and we all laughed.

It's boring to hang out while your kids grow up and ignore you. The most wonderful kind of boring in the world.

When I saw the way my father looked at my children, I knew with certainty that he had sat outside of my operating room praying. I knew he saw the burden I had been handed and said, "Give it to me, let me take it, let me carry some of it." I know it in my soul. I know it because that's the way I look at my children now and that's the way I'll always look at them until I die. That's what we don't know until we become parents. That is why everything changes and the world is a different place when you love your kids.

It is not a thing I do alone. It is a thing I do with help. At first, with nannies who changed in and out, and at last with a singular, extraordinary woman named Cathy. Cathy has continued to study while working with us. She has earned her master's degree in early-childhood education. She is an athlete, who had a scholarship in basketball. She swims like a demon. She is tall and strong and powerful and loving. She loves and protects my children with all of her might. She is our Alice in our unconventional Brady Bunch.

I know I'm good at night, less good in the early morning. I get help for the early morning. I know that after a stroke and with three children, I need good help to be the best parent I can be. That doesn't make me less; that allows me to do all of the things I do well. It allows me to do the important things. And I determine what those things are. Me, not the judgers.

If you should choose a path such as this or find yourself on a similar path, don't be afraid to ask for help if the resources are available to you. This is not a weakness and you will enrich others' lives by sharing yours with theirs. It can take a village.

Sometimes within that village, you are the prince or princess, sometimes the teacher or student, and some days, you might find that you are the village idiot. Those days are filled with so much humor and learning. Especially when your kids' little faces are there, turned up at you, smiling.

As they grow and we grow and the house fills out, I find myself amazed over and over again, and I wonder why I waited so long. Each day I look at them and they seem new. *I* seem new and it is extraordinary to think that I ever hesitated. I'm not saying three kids is easy. It's not. It's a lot of work. Being a single mom is a lot of work. And I don't think that society gives a lot of respect to the single mom. I don't care if you, like me, are a wealthy single mom. If there is no dad, people look down on you. When I go to work, I don't always get the same respect. I am very proud to have had the wonderful opportunities I've had and to have been successful in my life and in my career. I am very honored to have been able to share that success with my family. Yet when I work there are those who still behave as if I am abandoning my children. There still exists a double standard. Surprisingly, it is sometimes other women who apply this scrutiny.

I would have been very happy to have a good and devoted partner. But if I could do it again, maybe I would not have waited to put one before the other, or waited until my forties to have my kids, as I did. I think all of the societal judgments were so heavy in my generation that it held me up, even though I was a bit of a renegade. I didn't realize I was still trying to fulfill a picture of an idea that I had in my head. Or an idea that was developed centuries ago.

While Bob and I didn't stay together, he always demonstrated to me what it meant for a man to show up for me and to do the right thing, to be honest and good. I realized the other day that my children named nearly all of the childhood pets—all of the goldfish, mice, turtles, and one of our cats—"Bob." I thought it was so funny at the time; now I wonder if somehow they intuited that this was what we call love and caring.

No one can ever make your dream perfect but you. No one ever will. There will always be the detractors telling everyone how you could have done it better or differently. There will always be someone who thinks I was nuts to adopt three kids on my own. There will always be someone who thinks I work too much or not enough or in the wrong way or that I believe in the wrong things. There will always be someone who doesn't know how tired I really am. There will always be someone who doesn't know how much I really care. There will always be someone.

But at the end of my day, there will also always be my family: my beautiful family, my choice.

Karma

During the year of my fiftieth birthday, I went to the Cannes Film Festival, as I often did during my twenty-two years representing amfAR, to raise both money and awareness for HIV/AIDS. That year my cohost would be Madonna. I was quite pleased about that, as I like Madonna very much and admire her strength of character and her ability to accomplish so much in both her professional and her personal life. Her ability to help others while maintaining her family life and keeping her career relevant is a sensational accomplishment. We are almost exactly the same age, and I know that women of our generation did not come by this easily or accidentally.

We have often been pitted against each other, as this has been the way that the press and, I would have to say, society in general has found to bind women of our and past generations. There was not a place for women to find camaraderie, alliance, or safety with one another. It was put to us that there could be room for only one; that the only thing we might have in common was some man we might both want, have had, or be interested in having; that our competitiveness was something we could share, but only that. I must admit, I had fallen in line on some occasions with this belief, as there was no other one presented.

Over the years Madonna and I have had so many experiences while traveling somewhat side by side on our roads of fame, aging in public and so forth, that I feel close to her. I feel as if I secretly champion her. I know she feels the same. We stand up for each other without being asked. We know the pitfalls of being who we are and have been when we were breaking barriers in our respective fields. I have tried to learn from her at times and to empathize with her at others. The one thing I always have for her is love.

So I was over the moon, and nervous, to have this opportunity for us, for Madonna and I, to do this thing together.

I arrived on time and ready to go. I was the host, and I would be super-together. I would make her feel at home at all costs.

I got to the Moulin de Mougins, the hotel and restaurant of our host, Roger Vergé. He was the kindest and most respected chef of his area and in many parts of the world. We all loved him very much. My friends and I went to the Moulin other times as well, as this was our favorite place to gather, to laugh, to work out our plans for our charities, and to see one another.

On this particular night, as with all amfAR events, the street was lined with fans and French police. Per usual, I arrived by police escort, traveling the somewhat long drive from the Hotel du Cap-Eden-Roc on the French Riviera in a fabulous car that was donated for the evening. We sped along the coast and then up through the gorgeous countryside. I worked out my plans for the evening, opening my mind to a higher purpose, waiting to be directed by divine intervention, which I always count on.

I always think about how much money we raised at the event the time before, if I can make more this time, if I can beat the thirty-two million dollars I got out of the room at the last event, if this will be the year that changes everything. I worry about whether we will all be safe, if the threats will be handled, if the security will be on their game. I wonder if the cohosts will show up, if the musical guests will arrive, and if they will throw a fit or will be happy and the night successful. I wonder if I can send a police vehicle to pick up a friend who will grab his guitar, like my friend Wyclef Jean did: he just jumped in the cop car and came and played barefoot, because we needed him.

I wonder if we will get the big bids, if a prince will let me sit on his lap or a rock star will show us his underpants. I wonder if all of the shenanigans everyone has gone through to get the auction items into the country have in fact come together, as I know a lot of people have been up for weeks pulling off yet another major spectacle and that we are doing it for the benefit of those who so many do not believe in. I know we are swimming upstream and that we are doing it on a wing and a prayer.

I say a lot of prayers and do a lot of meditations and special little things that make me feel centered, no matter what it takes. Like putting my head down on the floor just to find six inches of quiet space to center myself in.

I remember the year the dresses didn't show up and Cavalli flew in replacements by helicopter, landing in the backyard of the hotel at the last second, their guy running up the lawn with forty dresses in his arms, covered in sweat. The time when the makeup artist didn't show up when expected because she was busy with a difficult star elsewhere. The period after my stroke when I couldn't see straight, the times when I made up things and mini-events to raise money impromptu. Like when Elton played with Ringo and Sam of Sam & Dave and some of my friends from the modeling industry and I sang backup. We all just threw ourselves at this, with love, and with the terror of continuing to fail. Or fail as I saw it, which was not finding the vaccine, the drug, the cure, the way to make it stop. Stop the pain, the dying, the crisis.

That car ride to these events was always my deep look inside. I would give myself over. I had to trust in the here and in the now. And no matter how crazy it went, how good or weird it was, how much we made, I always wanted to do better, to be better, to learn more, to move forward. To leave my own shame of failure behind, to find a way to succeed better.

And then I would get out of the car and act like a star, because, after all, that is my job.

That night, I arrived at the line of fans, who I always stop and see, shake hands with, sign autographs and take some pictures for. Then, with the aid of the police, I turned and began to work through the long and vetted line of global newspeople. I did filmed interviews for countries around the world on the current state of HIV/AIDS, both statistically and personally, for about an hour to an hour and a half, slowly walking down the drive while greeting arriving personalities, celebrities, royalty, local and global donors of extreme wealth and privilege, and the actors and actresses who gave us their support while at the festival promoting their latest work.

To this day I do this with the help and guidance of my long-time publicist, Cindi Berger, who took on this responsibility for free when we were both asked to step up with amfAR many years ago. When I first met Cindi, she was an assistant publicist. I had been offered other publicists, but I didn't connect with them. Pat Kingsley, who I adored, said she had a girl in New York who she thought I would hit it off with, "but she is on the other coast." Well, I was from "the other coast," so I thought that might be a good idea. We were a match. Cindi arranged for me to be on the cover of the "Hot" issue of *Rolling Stone* before *Basic Instinct* came out, which was no small feat. She put her growing career on the line for me.

As things went along in my career, she kept being promoted, had more clients, among them the Dixie Chicks. I was so proud of her when she stood up with them as they took so much heat for not supporting George W. Bush and his move into the wars that we are still in. Cindi made history when she put them on the covers of magazines instead of asking them to apologize, instead of making those women stop expressing their true beliefs. Today Cindi and those women stand on the right side of history, and today Cindi Berger is the chairman and CEO of the PMK*BNC public relations firm.

Cindi is the reason that all of the press and all of the world arrived for amfAR's galas. She changed the course of HIV/AIDS and is an unsung hero and has been and is my partner in all that I have done. As was her employee and my day-today person, Danica Smith. Danica worked hard and devoted herself with equal enthusiasm and care to everything amfAR.

Anyway, that year, the year I turned fifty, I had finally reached the end of this press line when Cindi got pulled away to deal with another issue. Madonna had not arrived. She was quite late. As she had not arrived at the party in her honor on Barry Diller and Diane von Furstenberg's yacht the day before, we were all beginning to panic. What if she simply doesn't come? While I don't know exactly what happened in Madonna's world that disallowed her to come to the party on the boat, I do know that Barry and Diane allowed me to turn this into a pre-fundraiser for amfAR. Then I asked the then-head of amfAR, Kenneth Cole, and his notorious sidekick at the time Harvey Weinstein if we could use this money to help fund pediatric research for HIV/AIDS treatment in China, as this year our other co-host was Michelle Yeoh and our attention was on China. I got the okay from all of them and then I got promises for two million dollars on that boat. We all had a great time and arrived at the event the next day even more anxious to see Madonna. As the French say, "Never go to your audience, make them come to you."

So Cindi was dealing with Madonna's absence when this unvetted Chinese journalist jumped me. He said something, which I never fully heard or understood, leading me to say, "At first, I'm not happy about the way the Chinese are treating the Tibetans. . . . And then all this earthquake and all this stuff happened, and I thought, 'Is that karma, when you're not nice that the bad things happen to you?'"

Yes. I said this. And yes, I was not and am not happy with

the way the Chinese treat the Tibetans. I am not happy with the way large parts of the world are treating one another, to be honest. I am not happy with the way my own country treats people. Anyway, this statement was not solely about the Chinese government and was not directed at the Chinese people. But this "reporter" meant to create scandal, and he did. He was not vetted, was not there for the benefit of amfAR or for HIV/AIDS.

When I said I was thinking, "Is that karma?" I was. I was thinking about that. It was not meant to be an accusation, but a thought. "What is karma?" In my own country we had the disaster with Hurricane Katrina in New Orleans, where we also were completely unprepared—we were not at all prepared to take care of our own people.

Hillary Clinton came out to L.A. to talk to a group of celebrities about what we could do to help. All of us, sitting on someone's living room floor: we were of course captivated by her. She said, "You all have special talents, talents I don't have: you can make movies, write songs, do all kinds of artistic things to change the world and it is so important that you do that." I was compelled to follow her lead.

I wrote lyrics with some young songwriters named Mark Feist and Damon Sharpe, who then got a great song composer to come on board and work with us: Denise Rich came on and pulled it all together and taught us how to make it work. So many amazing artists came together: from John Legend to The Game, from Céline Dion to Joss Stone, from Ruben Studdard to Gavin DeGraw—the list goes on and on. And this song became the title track for the album *Come Together Now,* which raised money for Katrina survivors.

For me, this is what I was thinking about with respect to China: What do we do about what has happened? What do we do about what we have done?

However, when someone wants to make scandal, they do. I felt used. I was prepared to host and greet so many important people, people who were there to make change, and I did; I was prepared to do fifty interviews to detail current HIV/AIDS statistics, and I did: that was my job. I was ill prepared for an unvetted, ill-intentioned man with a video camera to jump out and ambush me and twist my off-the-cuff thoughts regarding the Chinese earthquake into something bad or disrespectful.

Already I had been contacted by the office of the Dalai Lama asking me to lend my name in support of the earthquake relief effort that was happening at the Tibetan/Chinese border, as His Holiness obviously could not lend his. I did, and I was humbled to do so. We were interested in offering aid to the earthquake victims. Why was there a need to discredit me? I don't want to make up a story about why, because I will be wrong.

Cindi came back, and we moved to the black-tie-clad, huge wall of still photographers, who would get the photos out to magazines and papers all over the world. These people have changed the face of HIV/AIDS with their spectacular coverage of these events.

And then Madonna made her appearance. She is so tiny that you cannot believe the force of her tiny self. And though I am twice her size, I cannot sing a note. We had a ton of fun that night. She is a serious professional and had people hammering her for her time and attention, as she does constantly. We at amfAR were and are so grateful for her time and energy. Personally, I am inspired by her will, her dedication, and her humor. Together that year, we raised more than eight million more dollars for research in China.

From Cannes, I went on my own to the Karolinska Institute in Sweden, where I went to study with some of the top researchers in the world. About thirty doctors and research scientists and I sat around the table, each of us with our microscopes, discussing this tough topic.

I was there when, all of a sudden, my phone was blowing up with the news that I had inadvertently offended the country of China. Good Lord, how could I have offended a whole country? I did not want to participate at all. I did not want to respond and take my attention away from trying with these doctors to move forward toward a cure and a vaccine. My priorities were not at all about playing in this political merry-go-round. We all know the only way out is to get off of it. Why get on?

When I took the Dior contract that so saved me and helped me build my family, I said, "I won't stop being a public activist, and that has to be okay." They had agreed. But now Dior was demanding that I apologize to China. Cindi was, without my permission, consulting lawyers, who, without my permission, were issuing statements of apology on my behalf—statements that I had not seen. This had become a global crisis. Of course, George W. Bush was where? In China. Oh, I was a sucker just waiting for a beating. I was the ignorant star who would be used to take the spotlight away from something, but what? Would I ever know? Would anyone?

I was confused about why I should apologize, because I had no idea what the heck I was apologizing for. I had used my name to help people get earthquake relief near the site of the earthquake, but suddenly I was the idiot who'd said the wrong thing at the right time.

Dior released a statement in Chinese that said: "We don't agree with her hasty, unreflecting remarks and we deeply regret them. Dior was one of the first international brands to enter China and has won the affection and respect of the consuming public. We absolutely do not support any remark that hurts the Chinese people's feelings."

I do think it is key here to notice that Dior released statements. As if Dior spoke for me. This was the way the world thought a woman should be treated and respected. As if I could not speak for or explain for myself. As if Dior owned my thoughts or that our business relationship involving skin cream trumped my independent thoughts and feelings, because this unvetted, ill-intentioned man misused me to create scandal while I was doing my job regarding HIV/AIDS.

I was offended by the way I was treated. By the way "handling me" was done. I fired the lawyer, and even Cindi and I had major issues—of course, well resolved now. She had been horribly pressured both by Dior and China, while doing *her* job for HIV/AIDS. Not exactly your everyday experience.

This does not change the gratitude I felt and growth I experienced working for and with Dior. These two concepts do exist together. This is what it means to be professional and expansive.

But when asked about #MeToo, I think of things such as this.

I wonder if a man would have been used like this. Every intention that I had, every action that I took, was in favor of China. Every action and every thought that I was having was about how all of us could be better as human beings.

Dior declined to renew my contract, to spare themselves the spectacle of firing me. I was blacklisted in China.

Where did the money go that I raised for China? Should we ask Harvey Weinstein?

Since I was never invited to an amfAR board meeting and was never given their notes during the many years of my investment in this work, I find it hard to imagine that the proceeds from my birthday fundraising ever made its way to China, especially after the blacklisting. Even though I was the face of amfAR, the majority of the information I got about their financials came from the internet and from a woman named Bennah Serfaty, who worked there and would send me a few one-pagers just before events and nothing else at all.

I eventually apologized to the people of China, saying, "Due to my inappropriate words and acts during the interview, I feel deeply sorry and sad about hurting [the] Chinese people. I am willing to take part in the relief work of China's earthquake, and wholly devote myself to helping affected Chinese people."

Will China continue to blacklist me? I hope not. I have so enjoyed my visits there. I still have the rouge given to me by the lead character actor from a Chinese opera I saw and loved. It bonds me to the theater there. I think of the food, which I enjoyed so much, and the extreme beauties of the culture: one side of the street with a man in a rickshaw and the other with the most complex multistory electronic billboard I have ever seen. It is key to visit places to know what you are talking about. I miss learning more about China and its cultural heritage, I miss the opportunity to take my children, who are so bright and interested in the world, to visit. I believe that we all miss out when we close our minds and borders to global understanding of one another. We all have so much to learn and to share with one another when not in an imaginary conflict, created by artifice and fear.

My desire is to relieve the pain and agony of all of our children who are suffering from this dreadful illness, my desire is to be better and be of service. This was in no way disrespectful—or affected or changed by this event.

Hope

For more than twenty years I've helped raise money for sleeping bags for the homeless in downtown L.A. with my sister and our organization Planet Hope. We take the bags to the worst areas and throw them out of the backs of huge cube trucks with the help of some of the Los Angeles Rams—who can *really* throw—to thousands of homeless people. Kelly, Mike, Pat, Dad (before he passed), and I would take the responsibility to walk the bags under the bridges, up onto the sides of the reservoir, where people live in the holes, onto the AIDS street, where the worst cases all live together and others do not go in. Pat and I do that together, since these are all people who have had no treatment, so there can be quite a bit of mental illness there from the pain and suffering. One sex worker with HIV/AIDS always asks me for an extra bag. I always help her out. Her pain and suffering is something that touches the tenderest part of me.

The guy at the opening of the chain-link fence there always puts a tie on over his sweatshirt and says, "I knew you would come," though we don't always. The police have shut us down. In fact, one policeman shut me in the cube truck and tried to line up all of the homeless people, thinking he could create order. I sat inside in the dark on the metal floor, wondering if I would go to jail, if I would need to call my lawyer. Eventually the policeman opened the door. There were at least ten police cars lining the street beside our truck, and all of the cops were out, just leaning on their doors. That cop handed me his bullhorn. "Get them in a line—keep them off of the street." I got the drift that his own attempt hadn't worked out too well, especially once he realized that they would all love to be arrested, sleep in a cell with a blanket, and get a hot meal.

I made the effort, letting him know I respected authority. In my way. At least so that we could get these people somewhere to sleep. We passed out the bags, tried to make them stand in a line, as lines seem to make some people feel safer. I can say that when four- and five-year-old kids are being trampled by adults for a sleeping bag on Christmas Eve day, safety is not their first concern. Los Angeles has thousands of people on the street. Kids in the street, little tots in the street. In fact, in greater Los Angeles on any given night, there are more than ten thousand homeless kids.

They want us to rent a parking lot. They've asked us to get the people to stand in line, to make tickets for bags so we know who's gotten them. They've asked us to organize chaos among those fighting to stay alive. One has to wonder if they see the people or just the idea of the people.

My point is, this does not change country to country. This

does not change culture to culture. Is it convenient to help these people or more convenient to simply let them die?

When Kelly was working as a nurse in L.A., she worked for an orthopedic surgeon, a very popular doctor with athletes; football players who wiped themselves out on the field were one of his specialties. During the time she worked for him, he was getting older and had had a stroke, one he didn't reveal at work, as he wanted to keep going without that stigma.

My sister fell down the metal stairs outside at her job. She tore something in her leg and needed surgery. Her boss said he would do it. He was meant to make a vertical cut but made a lateral one instead, cutting her arteries and all kinds of stuff inside her leg, and then sewed her up. Within a few days it became apparent that something was terribly wrong: she had lost all feeling from the knee down. Kelly called for the videos of the surgery to see what had happened. It was too late to repair the damage; she would never again regain the feeling. She had many surgeries and lots of issues walking and was in danger of losing her leg.

She went back east to have an eighteen-hour surgery. The complexity of the surgery, coupled with her being under anesthesia for so long, made it extremely dangerous. My parents went with her. She survived the surgery but was in excruciating pain and was confined to a wheelchair with an enormous brace on her leg.

She was descending into a dark place. She was taking pain pills and her depression was mounting. We were all terribly worried about her.

At the time I was volunteering at a halfway house for teenage girls who had been tried and convicted as felons but given a second chance to live and be educated there. The stories of what they went through, living on the street, and what drove them to where they were had touched me immensely. After a kid is left on the street, within two weeks the kid is forced into prostitution to survive. There are statistics that support this, it's not my opinion.

I decided to take Kelly to the halfway house for her birthday. She was becoming addicted to the pain pills and I didn't want to lose her. She was more than unhappy about my choice, but I got her and her chair in the car for the six-thirty dinner.

Those girls are tough; they are not soft, as no one was ever soft to them, but they are honest and real, and Kelly needed to see that there were girls who needed her and who didn't care what she was going through, as it was nothing compared to what they had been put through. She stood their test.

At the end of dinner, I announced that she would run their summer camp. She was furious. How could she do that? She couldn't even walk. She took the information, but she just was through with me.

She asked my mom to come out to Los Angeles. She made an agreement with Mom that she wouldn't take any pills until she got the work done in the a.m. and physical therapy done thereafter. She toughed it out for those girls. She got it done. Then she realized that she couldn't run the camp from a wheelchair, as it took place in the mountains of Malibu, and got herself up and walking with forearm crutches by the time summer camp started.

I ran the "medical" office, which meant I de-liced all of the kids with elbow-length rubber gloves I bought at a sex store and listened to their stories when they couldn't sleep at night. Some of those stories haunt me still.

When they got back on the bus to leave camp, one of the little girls, who was about ten years old, had a panic attack in the aisle on the bus, kicking and screaming and crying. We took that beautiful blond girl off the bus. My sister and I looked at each other; we understood.

It took several tries before we could get her on the bus. They drove away.

Kelly and I looked at each other. She said, "I can do better than this."

I said I would raise the money if she would run a camp of our own. So we started Camp Planet Hope, first for homeless kids and then for homeless kids and their mothers, who generally slept outside and in the alleys of the shelters in old appliance boxes, leaving the beds inside for their children.

We got medical buses supplied from Cedars-Sinai hospital with the help of Michael Douglas's family, and eventually dental buses supplied by my friend Dr. Jay Grossman, with whom we started Homeless Not Toothless. This allows homeless kids to have the dental care they need to go to school, and homeless adults to have their dignity and health. We now have every kind of dental care, and every type of dental specialist, all volunteers.

William H. Macy and his wife, Felicity Huffman, helped us raise the funds. We are all complicated as we learn how to become transparent.

This camp has turned around the lives of so many, including Kelly, who broadened and deepened her charity work. She has given shoes to migrant worker families and coats to impoverished families with the help of Burlington Coat Factory, which gives us seconds and unsold coats for families across our country whose children would otherwise share coats and miss school days to do so.

Kelly took her employees to New Orleans during Katrina and did the small, lifesaving things, like providing insulin to diabetics and eyeglasses to people who couldn't see otherwise, and helping the soldiers who were working day and night. Every year she gives tens of thousands of gifts, provided by Hasbro, to individual children in shelters. She provides unsold and seconded prom dresses and older rental tuxedos to schoolkids who would never get to go. This is just one of the important things my sister has done and does. I raised the money for many years; now she has a group of women who run the organization for her, as she has lupus and suffers its many complications.

We are now so blessed to have the help and support of her husband and my closest friend, Bruce Singer, who is right out there on the front lines, whatever it takes, opening their home to events, wrapping gifts, speaking to authorities, helping with legal matters—as he is a lawyer and gives us legal counsel for free.

I can also say that when Kelly is too sick to come with me, Bruce takes me to the tough stuff: to speak at the Hague, to address the U.N., to fight for what is right. It is Bruce who stands with us, with me, with Kelly. It is he, since we lost Dad, who heads our family.

A few years ago I couldn't be present for the annual Planet

Hope gift-wrapping party, where we normally wrap thousands of gifts for kids in shelters in Los Angeles. We receive donated toys and gifts from people we've tortured—I mean, asked relentlessly—for help throughout the years. They give us toys, games, basketballs, makeup, nail polish, iPods, anything that kids, babies to age eighteen, would enjoy receiving for the holiday.

Then we—all of our friends and volunteers—meet, usually at Kelly's, and we have stations set up with the names of several shelters on huge boxes. On the tables are clipboards with the names of the kids and their ages and the shelter they are in. Each person has to choose an appropriate gift for that kid, wrap it, put the kid's name on it, and put it in the correct box. This way, that child knows that they have not been forgotten. This can be a one- or two-day event. We do eleven to twelve thousand gifts, generally. The shelters send cube trucks to pick up as we call. The year I couldn't come, Laird, who was then thirteen, offered to make the speech to all of our volunteers on my behalf. I was so delighted, and I could see that he was chuffed.

I think about the places my family has traveled, the holidays and experiences we have shared. Often, I find myself thinking back to that Thanksgiving at the hospital in Arizona and the astonishing compassion that those two babies, both horribly sick with AIDS, had for each other.

These things, all of these small moments, days lived out with curiosity and willingness to serve, lead me to a better shore. It could seem like one thing or another was the life-changing moment that opened me to an understanding of myself. . . .

Really, I am still working to know. Touching life in the heart, reaching back when life reaches to me, that is what I try to do. There was a time when I first became famous when everywhere I went someone asked me for something. I was so overwhelmed. Which thing should I do, how could I possibly keep up, who was real and who was simply taking advantage of my newfound wealth of opportunities?

I decided to do whatever I was asked to do first. Eventually I didn't want to get out of bed. It was too much. Then I realized I had to surrender: to myself, to a more loving, dedicated me. I had to avail myself to myself, to a better self. Then I would know where and when I was needed and when I could truly help.

Oh, sometimes I continue to step on my tongue or go where I shouldn't, but all in all, there is so much work to be done. There are so many children to be fed, homeless to be sheltered, schools to be built, kids to be hugged, stories to be heard, people far from home, that I have found my days seem to fill themselves.

Fortunately, my dear friend and my oldest son's godmother recommended a woman to be my assistant. Now, thirteen-plus years later, Tina, my "work wife," has made all of this possible for me. She is the key: she organizes and suggests, she comes with stories of folks in need, people who we should consider helping or hooking up with people we know who could help. We have created a kind of switchboard help network. Of course, I personally cannot do everything that is asked of me, of us, but we can sometimes find someone else who can.

We have tried to do things and found out that the system itself won't let us. It is illegal to put bathrooms and shelters at the Mexican border for immigrants—in fact, it's a felony. One year we tried to pay off all of the layaways at the biggest department store in the poorest county in America at Christmastime. They wouldn't let us. It seems they like it when people just can't do it and they get their stuff back.

Helping is tough; there is a lot of red tape. Tina has an unbelievable memory for numbers and people, I have a memory of places and things. We are a good team. We get it done. When they let us.

Yes, it is rewarding. Kelly got her most recent medical treatment from a nurse who had previously been one of our mothers at Camp Planet Hope. We had gotten her and her child off the street and turned around. Just look at her now.

The Bull

I realized how much I loved my dad the first time he danced right up to death's door. He got diagnosed with esophageal cancer and was given a 3 percent chance of living three months. Well, our family, being 85 percent Irish, all had a big laugh about that. My stroke and my own grim-reaper waltz were only a couple years in the past, and anyway, we were already quite familiar with death by then.

Once, when I was in my thirties, I went home to visit my folks and took their white Caddy out to see some friends over at the country club, which was about an hour away. The road to the club ran directly down into the lake with a big wooden billboard, just like you are imagining. Well, I hit black ice, and there is no driving on that—you just have to pump the brakes and try to direct the car where you want to crash. As I didn't want to go into the lake, I lined up to hit a nearby telephone pole. I got so much velocity from the ice that when I hit . . . Well, I must digress here: I had been trained by my stunt double Donna Evans to crash a car, so before I hit, I lined up with the pole, took my hands off the wheel and my feet off the pedals, crossed my arms across my chest, took a big deep breath, and exhaled on impact. I hit the pole so hard it spit the Caddy in two. It pushed the engine into the cassette player, which pushed itself into the tape. The tape started to play, and it scared the shit out of me. I looked up and the pole was hanging, broken in two, over the windshield, bouncing from the telephone wire.

I opened the giant car door and got out. The car was totaled but I didn't have a scratch on me. Thank you, Donna Evans, world's greatest stunt double. She did all of the crazy driving in *Basic Instinct,* by the way. I asked her later why she pulled out in front of that oncoming semi on the highway to Stinson. She said, "Oh, I knew I could make it." She was the coolest, best stuntwoman and the kindest, nicest person every single time we worked together, and it was often. It still is.

Anyway, I called my dad and said, "Hi, Dad. I just totaled the Caddy."

He said, "Oh, I knew I should have driven you in this weather. I'll come and get you." Just like that.

So now I was in my forties, and he had cancer. What could we do but laugh? We're Irish-American and that's what we do. We told him to wear his tuxedo to wash the car so he could get some use out of it. We would come to breakfast and say, "Oh, hey, are you still here?" Yet in our own way, we were also serious. Everyone got a job. Mine was that he and Mom were going to move in with me.

When they arrived, I walked next door to the guesthouse I had built for them. My dad was pacing. I sat down on the couch and he sat down and put his head in my lap. I have never been so stunned in my life; my dad was the kind of guy who hugged like he might break you in two, but no tenderness . . . till now.

I was frozen; I didn't touch him. So many years of not knowing how. I just looked down as he began to speak. "What are we going to do?" he asked me. Like I knew, like all of my faith and holistic healing, good eating, exercise, meditation, and prayer could save him now. As if he hadn't thought I was an asshole all of these years as I searched for the truth, the light. God, I hoped like hell he was wrong.

Tentatively I put my hand on his shoulder. "Well, Dad, I may not be the person who can help you," I said, as I couldn't put my sudden confusion away fast enough to serve him. "But we will get you the right people. You can beat this, but you will have to believe it and you will have to be willing to put down your old belief system."

He got up and paced around. He looked at me and rubbed the back of his neck. "I'll drink monkey piss if I have to." I suddenly realized that maybe he had more faith than I did.

My dad, who had started out like the Great Santini, and still looked like an elegant old-school Mob figure on the outside— he had ended up like Mr. Rogers on the inside.

The next day we went to our local medical center and received a confirmed diagnosis: yes, he was totally fucked. The doctors said that they would not be able to remove the tumor because it had penetrated the esophageal wall; unless the tumor somehow retreated back inside the esophagus, there could be no surgery.

He came home and looked at me: "Well, what are we going to do now, kid?"

I took a deep breath. "Well, Dad, if you have three months to live on the outside bet, I guess you have about a week to get the tumor inside the esophagus so they can do the surgery."

He looked at me with a steady gaze. "How do I do that?"

He had no experience with meditation, no experience with yoga or breathing or any of the Eastern healing arts. And no time to practice.

"Okay, Dad, here's what you are going to do. I want you to visualize your tumor, okay?" And he did. "Now make it a color and see it very clearly. Now every time you think about your cancer, and I mean every time, no matter what else you are doing, whether you are talking, walking, taking a pee, or sleeping, I want you to do this meditation. Are you ready?"

He said yes just as simply and as easily as if I had asked him if he wanted a Coca-Cola. "I want you to visualize pulling that tumor inside of your esophagus; just get it in there. Do you think you can do that?"

He said yes. He never asked how, or what if he couldn't, or what if he failed, or said he didn't understand. He said yes and he meant yes. That is the kind of man he was. Yes meant yes, and he did exactly everything the way he said he would.

I grew up with this man, who had said, "A man is only as good as his word," and he was. We were expected to be. Without exception. He didn't believe in contracts; he believed in his handshake and that of others. He believed that you looked someone in the eye when you talked to them and if someone

didn't, you knew that they couldn't be trusted. We were punished more for lying than for anything that we could possibly
have done wrong; in fact, if we came clean and were willing to
do it right or over again, we could avoid the punishment. I knew
I could count on him.

A week later that tumor was inside of his esophagus. Not
kind of in, not slightly moved; it was all the way inside. He
could have the surgery. He did it through meditation and sheer
willpower: a desire to live.

They told us that the most dangerous part of the surgery
is when they remove the esophagus and upper stomach; it's
then that the heart rate can plunge. I told my dad to make up a
meditation where his heartbeat was like a drum and to ignore
every other thing that was said or done in the surgery room. I
told him to ask them not to talk about other things during the
surgery, to be quiet other than the things that needed to be
said during the surgery. Only to beat his drum. He did it. His
heartbeat did not change at all during his successful surgery.
They called him the Bull. They have named a machine after
my dad at that hospital.

He had eighteen follow-up surgeries to stretch the opening
in his throat. The doctors told us no one beats this kind of
cancer. Every time he went in, he did a meditation to prepare
to win. At one of these appointments they called in advance to
say they had seen "something" in the scan, and he needed to
come in. He came over to my house to talk. He said, "What
do you think it is?" I said it didn't matter what I thought it
was, it mattered what he decided it was. But in my opinion, he

should decide it was something he could get rid of. I suggested he decide a trout swam up his ass while he was trout fishing. He laughed and went off to the appointment. He came home all smiles. "It was just some scar tissue," he said and winked at me.

Five years later, he was still cancer-free.

Then he was diagnosed with celiac, he was diagnosed with Alzheimer's, he was diagnosed with Parkinson's. I told him he had circled the drain more than Drano. Through it all, it is my belief that what my father truly had was love. The love of a good woman. Of course, she is my mom, steadfast and true, and a very interesting, smart, funny, beautiful nut. I have never seen a love like theirs: so vast and yet so sturdy.

He meditated through to the end. Transcendent, peaceful, without pain, even though his body was disappearing in front of us. Toward the end he looked like a ballet dancer: just bones and muscles. All of those years of lifting huge metal blocks as a die sinker, that big, macho, muscular body had come down to this.

He awoke from a coma to call for a kiss from my mother, his partner of sixty years. He was a practical man, a hardworking and naturally skeptical man, and in the end he deepened my faith by his example of God's goodness and of his own selfless integrity.

The lessons of my second life are of recovering from loss. The loss of all things we call dear: my father, my three closest friends, my marriage, my health, the custody of my son, my career, my financial stability—one might say my identity. The grief and sense of failure that this caused was terribly, awfully overwhelming.

The thing is, I didn't—I didn't lose.

In Buddhism one comes to learn and understand that complete emptiness has to come before renewal can happen. Not 59 percent emptiness, but total, complete transparency and full disclosure. This is what Richard Gere was talking about with "Gone, gone, gone. Gone, gone, completely gone. Enlightenment." This is where we become cleansed, and renewal can begin. In my case there was a total sense of going, going, going, gone—and with that a coming of light.

Our parents will pass on, and not at all when we are ready or not busy. I was busy—it's true—but guess what? Too bad. We will at some point lose our friends, and sometimes it will be horrific and sequential. In Hollywood there is a legend that we die in threes. When one person dies we all become paralyzed, waiting. I lost three women in just a few years. With the trauma of going through cancer with my warrior women, I feel like I get how war buddies must feel. You just can't explain it. It was so awful and so deep and bonding all at the same time.

For me, the first had been Marge. I didn't know Marge at all when we found ourselves standing in a circle of Hollywood's elite. It was the Oscar-hopeful party for *Casino* that Susie and Harold Becker had thrown for us. It was so glamorous, buzzing with excitement. There was a kind of oval of coolness with Marge at the far end. She was being quite funny, and I had heard she was a key writer for *Seinfeld*. I said to her, as we were all throwing out jibs and jabs, "Hey, what's with the bald head," to which she threw back, "Cancer." There was a pall of silence. We never broke eye contact. The rest of the oval shirked off and we started laughing like idiots.

I said, Wow, that is so interesting, I want to write a movie where I play Death, who wants to quit because nobody likes her, and you must think about dying all of the time—wanna write it together? That was it; we were inseparable.

You might think we wrote a great script, but no, she just proceeded to die, and I became one of two primary caregivers. The other being Kathleen Archer, who was a woman from Marge's neighborhood who noticed that Marge wasn't walking her dog anymore and came by to see why. We became a team and best friends for a time. A good and valuable time.

We went through some amazing times. The worst of those were the funniest. I don't know how Kathleen and I did it. My mother was such a big help. She had lost her closest friend, Elsie, to cancer back in those silent C-word days and never had another friend like that again. She understood.

Mom made the lemon meringue pies that Marge wanted on Oscar day. Marge couldn't eat anymore but she wanted to see them, to smell them. We took them over and I got in bed with Marge to watch TV. Suddenly the people on TV were going into the Oscars and I realized that I was supposed to be there. I was *nominated*.

"Holy shit, Marge, I have to go!!!" I screamed out.

"You, you, you, always *you*," she said with a laugh, as I ran out, shoes in hand, Mom running after me.

In the days leading up to the Oscars, Vera Wang and I had been working on a couple of dresses. We were experimenting with fabric and failing with some, winning with others. Ultimately it came down to two dresses. One of them didn't work because the fabric went kind of sideways, which was funny for us and creative, and we had the backup dress which did work. So Vera finished the winner and FedExed it out to me. It arrived the day before the Oscars, but as the driver took it out of the truck it fell off of the back and for some unknown reason, he backed over the box. It broke open as it happened, and he drove a big black tire track all of the way up the front of my pink Oscar gown.

I just picked it up and went inside, sat down, and cried. Then I called Ellen Mirojnick, who did all of the costumes for *Basic Instinct* and all of Michael's other movies. Ellen came and looked at the dress and at me and at the situation. I was presenting two Oscars with Quincy Jones. I was *nominated.* We just stared at each other.

"Okay, go and get all of your favorite things out of the closet," Ellen said.

"Black tie?" I asked.

"No, just your favorites."

So I got a whole lot of black clothes—that Johnny Cash impulse again—and put them all over my bedroom floor and Ellen started making them into outfits. We ultimately picked a ready-to-wear Valentino long black skirt, the now infamous Gap turtleneck, and a Giorgio Armani long black silk velvet tuxedo dress, which I opened and wore as a coat over all of that. I took a gardenia from my garden as my boutonniere. And my dad as my date, which seemed to make everything okay.

This thing, this turn of events, seemed not only to free me

but to free my inner artist, to know I was there not because of a dress or because of the show, but because of my work. I felt more grounded in that Gap turtleneck than I had in a lot of other hard-to-carry dresses. It taught me that comfort is the most important step to style.

The best part of this is that I did it with my friends. First with Vera Wang, who I started working with at the beginning of my career and in the transitional part of hers, when she moved from doing solely bridal to fashion. Then Ellen and I created a new kind of Oscar fashion together, and had fun and made a panic into an adventure.

All of this was a time when two of my friends were dying of cancer, when all of our friends were pulling together on everything. Even the Oscar days were a kind of moment that was deeper in meaning for this sense of women moving together and making the big, little things into acts of grace.

A few months after the ceremony, I was on the phone with Kathleen and the operator broke in. "I have an emergency call for Kathleen or Sharon." We knew this was it. Kathleen said, "Let me take it." I did. I had to go somewhere, I don't remember where now, but on the way back up my street in my convertible I looked in the rearview mirror and Marge was sitting in my backseat. And then she was gone.

I often made friends with people only to find out they were also from Pennsylvania. I made one really good friend in San Fran: Caroline. The first time we met, I heard her before I saw her: a voice with an accent very particular to where I grew up. "Ja eat jet?" she was saying. "Ja know I kilt a deer, I tied it to the ruf a my car, wanna see it? I got some pop in my truck." I started laughing so hard I was crying. It was like a secret language, a secret handshake from my childhood. I followed the voice and we were instantaneously devoted friends.

She was, like me, a middle-aged woman from Pennsylvania. She—a bright, funny, short-haired, fit lesbian living in San Francisco—was the person big businesses brought in to sort out their finances. If the books didn't make sense, they brought in Caroline and she got to the bottom of it, no matter what. She got a percentage of what she recovered. She was a financial wizard. She was hilarious, kind, and charming. The day we met, she was recovering the finances of the doctor who had saved her from breast cancer.

I was visiting that doctor's office for my first breast tumor issue. Just the way we were put together is a classic example of a godsend. Caroline thought she was going to be there for me—she thought she was going to be my advocate. As it turned out, my tumors, though difficult, were benign. Instead, I would end up being her advocate until the end. Because a couple of years later, Caroline came over to tell me her cancer had returned. She told me that at first she thought she had gotten giardia, an infection of the gut one can pick up from contaminated water. But no, she had picked up cancer again, in her stomach this time.

Roan wasn't even a year old at this point. I was holding him on my lap. I decided to just go straight to believing that we could handle it. Why waste time on all of the dramatics? He threw his little arms around her neck.

I was as present and as helpful as I could be. We shared so

much life, we practically moved into each other's houses. I had clothes at her house; she had clothes at mine. It was amazing. Caroline and I went to Hawaii near the end. We blew so much money staying at a private house on the golf course at one of the best hotels. Golfing in the cool afternoon breeze up until sundown. The whales jumping around, as it was during that gorgeous season. Getting back to the clubhouse at sunset, those luscious tropical sunsets, she would have a drink, I would have a toke and a tea. . . . She had no hair at all by then. I had shaved it off when it began to fall out. First in a labyrinth pattern, which she loved, then all of it. That's when she began to leave her Marinol pills and extra glasses and some jammies at my house. That's when we both knew it wasn't going well. That's when we knew we were walking toward the end of our journey.

She told my mother, "I'd be dead already if your daughter would just let up. But no, she has to just keep on nagging." We all laughed, out of some kind of protocol. My mother knew a thing or two about hard times and how to handle them.

Caroline died at home with her partner of many years, with me and my ex-husband on the phone trying our best to talk them through it. She reached out even then. She was like that.

Through it all, all those fast years, my head of security was a woman named Kristin. I first met her when she came as my limo driver to pick me up for an event. She was professional and kind, with beautiful, vibrant red hair. She was a fabulous driver, efficient, fast, safe, and tough. I asked her if she had security training and she said that she had. She mentioned having been a sheriff from a smaller town in Northern California, a Brinks truck driver, and a transporter of felony prisoners from prison to prison. I thought that was so cool. I asked if she still had a license to carry; she said that she did.

I hired her again and again, for months on end. She continued to amaze me with her professionalism and courage. Finally, one night I went to the Oscars, changed in the backseat, and then went to Elton John's afterparty. I came out in my brand-new flesh-toned, beaded minidress and new high heels and she was of course pulled up right near the front in our limo. I came out of the party so gassed up that I had been at these events that I was unprepared when the fans broke down the stanchions and rushed me. I began to run to the car in those new shoes and was just about to make it when I started to slide. It was clear I was going to hit my shins full-bore and slide right under the car; I couldn't stop. Kristin grabbed me by the back of my dress, two-handed, and picked me up and threw me headfirst into the backseat. She slammed the door, jumped in, and got us the heck out of there in the nick of time.

She did things like this regularly. We were at a Laker game just as laser sights were becoming popular, and someone put one on the back of my head. Kristin stood behind me facing the bleachers and it landed on her chest. Signaling for the head of floor security to get me out of there, she marched up those bleachers, throwing people left and right, keeping the sight on herself. She was going to find the bastard who was threatening me.

Another time I was receiving mail from a "fan" who was

writing strange and oddly threatening letters to me from up the California coast, declaring not only his love for but his dangerous attachment to me. No one, no agency, had been able to find him as the postmarks got closer and closer to my residence. Finally, I got one hand-delivered to my mailbox. I told Kristin to go and find him. She did. She found him in a campsite and walked up to him. She told him she came at my special request and needed to see his writing to be sure it was him. She compared the writing and then took him down and called the authorities who had been tracking him. As always, she got the job done.

In the beginning, when I hired a woman to be my head of security, we got a ton of shit everywhere from everyone. It seemed to be an offense that I thought a woman could handle this big job. How could she do this? She was ambushed by other people in her field. They slashed our tires. They put stuff in our gas tank. She never said a word. She simply repaired whatever they did and handled it all so elegantly and so toughly. She replaced our car or our tires or whatever happened without a word to me or anyone. Of course, I knew, but I let her carve out her own world.

All that I said was that she had to be learning in that front seat, every day and all of the time she wasn't driving. I didn't care what, as long as she was educating herself. You see, her dad had been a nuclear physicist for NASA and an abusive parent and partner. When she was a little girl—and I mean four and five years old—if she made a mistake, he would lock her out overnight and she would have to sleep on the front steps of their house. When he died of natural causes, a heart attack, they investigated both her and her mom because they were showing no visible signs of sadness.

This had made her tough on the outside, but she was still a softie on the inside, and of course brilliant. It was wonderful to spend fourteen years in the car with her. It would have been a lifetime for me—and was for her. She got neuroendocrine cancer when she was thirty-nine. She had particularly bad skin on her face. I sent her for tests, as we couldn't clear it up at the dermatologist. The tests came back showing that she had cancer. She had driven my dad every day to his chemo and the doctor there had fallen in love with her. Now handling her care, he called and said he thought the test was labeled incorrectly, because she was too young for this. He did the test again. He was crying when he called me back.

I was doing a guest spot on a show called *The Practice* when we found out. Kristin and her girlfriend came to the set to talk. I tried to be strong but lost my mind. They left and I didn't know what to do, so I let myself in to a storage closet, the only private place on the soundstage. I collapsed onto the floor amid a sea of paper towels and toilet paper. I was so lost, so heartbroken. She would die. The cancer was everywhere. It was a death sentence: they gave her only months to live.

Suddenly, without warning, there was a woman standing beside me. A beautiful black woman who said, "Sister, are you in need of prayer?" I was awe-stricken.

"Yes," I said.

She was holding a gigantic Bible. She simply got down on

the floor, put her hand on my head, and began to pray out loud. She calmed me and then she left as she had come. Without a sound.

I went back to the set and stopped at the craft service table to eat something and pull myself together. The craft guy had a hat on that said JOHN 3:16. I just looked at him. I had no idea what was happening. I'm not particularly religious, but even I can take a hint.

We, all of us who loved Kristin, did everything we could to help her. We did full-moon hoop ceremonies with an extraordinary Native American in Arizona. We did stem cell replacement. We did every single thing that anyone said could be done, no matter how woo-woo or impractical. We had nothing to lose. She lived for four years. We took trips. We made the most of it.

Some people didn't understand when I didn't go to her funeral. But this for me was not our gig. No, we talked about how to rob Brinks trucks and about all of the amazing things that she learned and taught me. She was like a daughter to me and I needed to grieve alone, not as a group and not as a spectacle.

There were times, though, like near the end, when she could no longer drive but still rode along, this time to the Oscars, when she got out of the car and opened my door, and all of the other bodyguards came and stood in a row behind her. . . . Times like those when we all stood for her, grieved together with our own understanding of who she was, who she showed them that she was. That was what counted. She earned dignity in their eyes and our respect.

We used to say that we knew this was not our first life together and that we had been burned at the stake together before. That this heat was nothing compared to that. I didn't replace her when she passed—I kept thinking I would, that another terrific, strong, tough woman would come along. I even asked the police to find someone, but there isn't one. There just isn't another Kristin. I suppose this was the thing that made me a bit of a recluse. I lost my wingman.

I still start crying when I think about hiring someone to permanently fill her position. I'll cry and pace around the room as I always have when I wanted to deal with my emotions. When I used to do this, Kristin would say, "What are you looking for?" while calmly sitting and watching me. One day I said, "My sanity." The next day she brought me a small box. Inside was a paper inscribed SHARON STONE'S SANITY and a butterfly, a real butterfly. Now, when I need to, I can walk over to the fireplace and open the box that sits on the mantel. It makes me feel at peace. There it is: my sanity.

My dad was a tough guy, but he also was a man who cried. Not often, but when things mattered. He also laughed until he cried, and often. He was willing to be vulnerable. Especially in his later years.

When he told me that he had learned to see the wonder in each and every day, that this was the kernel of truth, the key to wellness for him, he was then acknowledging that he had missed the obvious. He wanted to share this with those who needed it, and he spent the rest of his life doing that. Quietly and privately being present but putting himself in places where he was ready to be called to act. He stayed with Dot at the little house next door for months at a time.

He used to say he was going out for a walk and be gone all day. Eventually we knew what he was doing. He was waiting. Waiting for that someone who needed him. And they found him. There are men who step out of the most powerful and unusual places to say, "I met your dad," and then they tell me stories of how they ran into my dad—at the dry cleaner's, or in the park, or at the hardware store—and how he changed their lives just in the nick of time. There are rock stars and even a president of this nation who thought of my dad as their own. He did what he said—he saw the wonder in each and every day and showed others who had lost their way how to do the same.

When he was dying, they called him, talked to him, sang to him, and stood by his bedside to the end. They spoke at his memorial. Heads of the largest corporations in this country. My dad, an ordinary Joe.

Me Too

As I sit here now, nearly two decades later, the right side of my head still hurts. This is where the brain damage is, where the scarring is. My hearing is back, though sometimes I have to turn my head a bit to shut out the sounds that can interfere with what I am trying to hear. I am walking normally. I have all of the feeling again in my left leg, though getting it back was hell. Each stab of pain was a sign that that area was waking up, the excruciating stabs a stunning hello to a previously dead zone. I can write again; that took only a year or so. I was able to control the pen and keep it on the paper, though writing my own name was always the hardest. I often wondered if that was because I was now a different person. Was I no longer Sharon Stone, or simply no longer the Sharon Stone I had been before?

The stuttering stopped after about four or five months, when I was finally put on the correct anti–brain seizure medication. Same with the colored blocks that appeared in my vision, and the undulation of the floor beneath my feet. My depth perception returned.

My memory, both short- and long-term, took longer. I used

to have a near-photographic memory. Now I didn't know what the heck was going on. Over the years most of it has returned. Doctors and spiritualists say that the brain will work around damage, and I can say that in my experience that's true. It will find its own new pathways. The interesting thing is that as the injury's healed, I have found myself with greater perceptions than I had prior to my injury. In effect, I am now using more of my brain than before. I have learned how to access more of my own mind.

With that I have come to have both greater compassion and a realization that not everyone should receive that compassion. There are those who get up each day and choose to walk a bad road. That is their choice, and to waste one's compassion there is a dangerous path. One that I will not walk again.

This allows me to be both more pragmatic and more loving. This allows me greater spiritual safety. It is easier to see who is real and truthful and who is pretending for nefarious reasons. While it can feel lonely to realize this piece of life, it is important to spend this alone time, to find a deeper place within oneself.

It took many years and almost dying for me to work my way back to myself. But now that I am myself again, or this self again, I have a happy house, full of laughter and fun. When I just had my career, I worked hard only at that. I was very disciplined. But my home was empty. I loved my work and I had good success in my work. But my work did not love me back. When I had times of confusion or needed guidance, my work did not guide me or help me.

I recently had a talk with my European bodyguard, Bruno. We have traveled the globe together for more than thirty years. He was laughing, saying that when we started, his job was much more difficult since I was much more difficult. Of course, it was also at the height of my fame, which was a scene. But he said that the change in me from my Buddhist practices was so big that I had become, in his words, "so beautiful on the inside" and "so easy to be with," and so his job was easy now. I must have been a hellion. In fact, I am sure of it. I used to love to mix it up.

Peace of mind is a rush, though, I must say. Bigger than the other thing—and a lot less trouble. Though I can look back and laugh. Oh, I used to cause some trouble. I used to love to piss people off. Just to watch. It was so easy to wind people up. I think that I liked to have control of people's minds and it was so easy to get them off their rockers. I wasn't the person who was at home later thinking, *Gee, I wish I'd said that,* I was the person who went home thinking, *Gee, I wonder if I really should have left them in pieces on the floor.*

It is okay to change.

So, the acting thing: I do still like it. Actually, I like it more than before. I feel much more comfortable in it, and it's a whole lot easier to do. I feel less pressure when I do it now, as it is not my entire world. I have also had more profound life experiences to bring to it. When the workday is over, good or bad—and it's mostly always good—I go home to a house full of love, so no big deal.

I am not hungry for it. People can tell and they like you hungry. Jeez, do they like you hungry. This town is keen for the hunger. It's like a zoo at feeding time all day long. But Mama's a big animal, so I guess I could have that hungry look anytime. Maybe I could even have the *I could eat you* look. If you know what I mean.

I am proud of my success in my work. It belongs to me, I earned it. I kept getting up to bat, just like my dad said. Not every movie or TV job I've done has been a winner. Some of them seem like I'm a pie girl again: just shoveling the crap out of the can into the premade crust. However, work is work. I go into each project wanting to do my best, be my best, hoping for the best outcome. Hoping to be promoted. I get myself a little gift each time. A sweater for this job, a new kitchen for that job, the kids' tuition for this one, in rougher times. Each one is sweet, even if it didn't work out as a box-office hit or even if the thing as a whole failed.

Even with the worst directors, like the one who wouldn't direct me because I refused to sit in his lap to take direction. This #MeToo candidate called me in to work every day for weeks, when Laird was a brand-new baby, and had me go through the works—hair, makeup, and wardrobe—and then wouldn't shoot with me because I refused to sit in his lap and take direction. Yes, this was a multimillion-dollar studio film, of which I was the star, and the studio didn't say or do anything. I just kept coming to work and spending the day constantly getting retouched in my trailer and being with my baby.

Of course the film was a bomb. The level of insecurity and unprofessionalism and I would guess drug abuse required to make those kinds of choices never leads to good work. But as a superstar, which at that point I was, and a woman, I had no say. That was how it was in my day. Even a high, abusive director had more power than I did.

Thank God it is not that way now. The whole system is changing. The financial burden is real, and the old boys' club isn't covering for this anymore. There are more women at the helm, and they aren't in the pocket of the men, forced to play along or be canned.

Not to say there weren't great men in my day too. Men who would come in and shut the show down when things were going wrong, men who would talk to me. Those men helped us make great pictures. Those men helped us make great pictures like *Casino*. Those men shut down a show I was on when the director was so high on cocaine he was spinning. Now that same director has sobered up and gone on to do fabulous and important work. Not with me, of course, as I aided in the shutdown.

I don't regret my choices. Being an actress used to be everything to me. Really, just everything. I used to eat, sleep, breathe, run, play, and work at nothing but acting. I loved everything about it. The pages of words, the look in the other actors' eyes, the lost places in the scenes, the scents of the soundstages and locations. The feeling of pulling up to a new location, like running away with the circus. I was putty in the hands of a great director, thrilling to his every thought, and angry to be held hostage by the mediocre ones.

I loved working for the studios, feeling the tradition of the ones who went before me: Bogie and Bacall, Tracy and

Hepburn, Sidney Poitier, Lena Horne, Gene Kelly and Fred Astaire. I wanted to be great like they were. I wanted to be a super-pro. I wanted every movie to be a hit; I worked my ass off to sell my movies all over the world to make sure they were. I was proud to do it, happy to be a studio girl.

I stood up for gay actors and actresses; I told the studio when their people were not available to work because they were too high to talk or too drunk to drive. I was on the side of the studio, and I loved my job. That didn't work out great for me either. It's not a popular position to be in: certainly not then, certainly not as a woman. It would be fair to say I fucked myself.

Now, I suppose in retrospect, I might seem dependable. I was the one who always sold my films, good or not so good. Showed up to work on time, did my job. But then, in the good ol' days, with the good ol' no-rules, women as superstars were not a darling of the system. They preferred us to be ornaments. I was supposed to do what I was told.

I had actor approval in my contract. No one cared. They cast who they wanted. To my dismay, sometimes. To the detriment of the picture, sometimes. I had a producer bring me to his office, where he had malted-milk balls in a little milk carton–type container under his arm with the spout open. He walked back and forth in his office with the balls falling out of the spout and rolling all over the wood floor as he explained to me why I should fuck my costar so that we could have on-screen chemistry. Why, in his day, he made love to Ava Gardner on-screen and it was so sensational! Now just the creepy thought of him in the same room with Ava Gardner gave me pause. Then

I realized that she also had to put up with him and pretend that he was in any way interesting.

I watched the chocolate balls rolling around, thinking, *You guys insisted on this actor when he couldn't get one whole scene out in the test. . . . Now you think if I f— him, he will become a fine actor?* Nobody's that good in bed. I felt they could have just hired a costar with talent, someone who could deliver a scene and remember his lines. I also felt they could f— him themselves and leave me out of it. It was my job to act and I said so.

This was not a popular response. I was considered difficult.

Naturally I didn't you-know-what my costar; he was baffled enough without me confusing him some more. But he did make a few haphazard passes at me in the upcoming weeks, I'm sure spurred on by this genius.

I've had other producers on other films just come to my trailer and ask, "So, are you going to f— him, or aren't you? . . . You know it would go better if you did." I take my time and explain that I am like the nice girl they grew up with, and get them to recall that girl's name. This leaves us all with a little bit of our dignity.

Sex, not just sexuality on-screen, has long been expected in my business. I do not in any way think that this is about my business, particularly. I have seen my mother in a rage because some man pushed her up against the filing cabinets at my dad's factory. I have heard her in the kitchen saying, "I told that bastard to back the fuck up before I stick him in the neck." Then we all laugh at her and with her. But I know how scared she felt.

My father used to call me back from playtime in our giant yard, take me aside, and, putting his hand on my shoulder, say, "You are letting those boys beat you so that they will like you. Now, go out there and win, and they will respect you."

While my dad made me strong and he made me tough, and this protected me from a sea of ravages, it also put too much armor around my femininity. It has taken the #MeToo moment for my mother and I to talk and for me to gain the perspective of my true feminine power and the glory and beauty of it.

For my generation of women, this could be seen as good-naturedly spilling the milk shake I was serving onto the lap of the asshole who put his hand up my skirt as I worked my way through college in blue-collar Pennsylvania.

Roy London suggested I approach my male bosses with my "feelings," so as not to be threatening. He said they would be less threatened if I had "feelings" instead of opinions. I tried that. Tried so long to keep working without compromising myself.

People used to say, "Sharon Stone has the biggest balls in Hollywood." It's not a coincidence that I was the first woman to get paid something considered respectable—still a whole lot less than men, but more than women had been paid in the past.

People criticize me and say that men are intimidated by me. That just makes me want to cry.

I was often alone on a set with hundreds of men. Hundreds of men and me. Often not even the caterer employed women when I was first working. My makeup and hair were men. Can you imagine what it was like to be the only woman on a set—to be the only *naked* woman, with maybe one or two other women standing near? The costumer and the script gal? And now *I* am the intimidating one.

This new press circus, with the humble letting go of the accused with a tidy yet massive settlement, is not due process for what are in fact crimes, crimes for which we have not discovered practical jurisprudence. Why must we "stand together and stay strong"? Where is the law? Did we let our pussy-grabbing president take that with him too? I personally do not believe that we did. I believe that there is a great and good court of law for this that must be revised, reviewed, revamped, reclaimed, and reconsidered to respect the sexuality of the public as a whole.

I know that all of these women and men who have been harassed, been raped, had their jobs held for ransom, and been sexually tormented deserve their day in court. I know that to be true. I know that all of the unprocessed rape kits on police shelves everywhere must be processed so that crimes can be solved. This inaction is a true and real crime in itself.

To some of the less violent trespassers of my personal space—the ones who have threatened to fire me if I didn't put out, for example—I suggested recently that if they would only sit with me and talk it out, I would let it go, without revealing their offensive behavior. I believed that a kind of truth-and-reconciliation discussion might be a good start. But so far, not one of them has manned up. It seemed like a more-than-fair offer, considering the humiliating and offensive state of my workplace. We must begin somewhere. There were always beasts. They weren't always men. We tried to stay out of their way. There were always perverts. We tried to warn one another.

A friend told me a story about another dear friend of ours who was driven by a guy out into a field, where he violently forced her to give him oral sex. She came home fractured, devastated. Her girlfriends sent her back out into that field with him again, this time with a container of Krazy Glue; yes, he did it again, and yes, she squirted the Krazy Glue into his pants and ran for her life.

I have worked with great men, great creative geniuses, good, decent, fun men, flirtatious, delightful men, men and women who I would trust with my life, and have.

So that is why I accept apologies, that is why I hear both sides of every story; I want due process, I want to stand up for the good ones, the wounded and the disbelieved on both sides. I believe in all of what is happening now. The law, not just the press, needs to get in gear on this. This time, this generation, the government, needs to listen to us, all of us.

I don't think that payoffs and Krazy Glue and shouts of "Fake news!" should be the way this continues to go. Do you?

Many people ask me what it was like in my days of being a superstar. It was like this. Play ball or get off the field, girl.

My work reflects the times when I did have the opportunity to collaborate with the good and great directors and I sat at their feet, learning everything I could for the times ahead. For I was not the chosen one, not the golden gal, just the sex symbol who could sometimes get the key part if she also happened to be sexy.

Then I did my best to make it count.

There is something that happens when you start over, live again. A kind of mystery unraveling.

There is an exercise in a book I read by Pema Chödrön, an American woman who became a Buddhist nun, where you sit and concentrate on that which is overwhelming you and ask this energy, this thing, to overwhelm you totally; to consume you. At the point of total consumption, then you ask how many others are feeling this same exact thing at the same exact time and you ask to join their energy. I have found this to be the most healing and compassionate exercise.

I have asked to be overwhelmed by the need to heal myself with love and to join those who feel the same. This sense of being overwhelmed and the sense of compassion and relief has been fuller than it has with the other meditations.

This reckoning, this journey, this written admission, has healed, is healing, my relationship with my whole family, but especially my mom. We all, in our family, had kept secrets of shame and terror, that threat of "sure death if we told" always hanging like the Sword of Damocles over us. We told ourselves and one another that we were protecting ourselves. Instead we lived in a fantasy, lacking fellowship and compassion—and, worse, one another.

It took years of therapy and reading, it took the world changing, it took #MeToo, to even begin to imagine that we, that I, could tell our horrible truths. Even then, who would I tell? How could I unravel a family from its suffering—not just mine, but quite literally a world of suffering?

I went to this seminar called *A Course in Miracles*. There was a workbook, the whole thing. The woman who taught this particular course, Marianne Williamson, was a wonderful teacher. I love a good teacher. She was sound, thoughtful, and sensible, and nothing she said seemed sensational. And I should say not at all like she came across in her presidential run.

We would meet, if I remember correctly, once or twice a week in a giant hall. There were hundreds of attendees. About halfway through this it dawned on me that it must have been hell for my grandfather to be a pedophile. I mean, who would get in that line? It occurred to me that anyone would jump in the give-me-terminal-cancer line before that line. That is a hideous destiny.

I realize it is hard to accept this thought about a pedophile. Don't get me wrong: it isn't compassion. It is forgiveness for the dead. If he was alive I would expect him to be in jail.

It then occurred to me that now that he *was* dead, he was free of his illness, free to be his divine soul and self. That whatever you believe God to be, God forgives, God loves, God accepts, and God heals. That now, now that he was free of his earthly sickness, I could be open to experiencing that freedom too.

That opened me to understand that we can forgive anyone just about anything when we separate them from their issues, illnesses, and faults. When we step away from the dangerously ill, and criminally insane, and make laws to get them the help, healing, and quarantine that they may need.

I understood something very difficult for me to understand. Very hard for me to accept. I understood it, I forgave it in this case. But I couldn't set myself free.

I couldn't trust this idea that I could be safe in an unsafe world. It did not make sense to me yet.

What I am now finding out is that I had to give myself some alone time. I had to meet my mother as a person, separate from my childhood experiences and judgments of her, and know her from an adult perspective.

I wanted out of my childhood world so badly. I wanted out of poverty and women having no voice. I wanted out of dreams that I couldn't even talk about without being made fun of. I wanted to be able to say what I thought and have someone know what I meant, what I really meant. I didn't want to always be the last one picked, the eccentric one, the different one.

What I did want was a place to be accepted. I wanted a world where a woman could be accepted equally and fairly.

I was so determined that, in my desperation, I forgot to notice that my mother would also so have loved someone to talk to. It was only after she and my dad came to live with me that she told me about being given away. Before understanding this, when my mother would come to visit and criticize my home, I thought she didn't like me. When I was able to afford a housekeeper, and then a daily housekeeper, my mom would talk more to them than to me. I didn't understand until much later that my mother, who had worked as a maid from the age of nine, found camaraderie with them. I didn't realize that I was often rude to my mother, as mean to her as she had been to me.

I had to face my own truths, so many of them not what I would like the world to see about me, or us. Yet we all make up stories about one another: when we don't know someone, we just make it up. I see that, I see the way I did that.

My mother is a survivor. My mother's childhood was not at all what I had imagined. Her life was not any of the stories I made up to survive. First I thought she had simply suffered from painful poverty; then I thought she had been sexually abused and been given away to get her away from that horror. And that somehow the madness of all of that had allowed her to leave us with her perpetrator. That she had run to my father at sixteen to escape whatever life she was having. She seemed to hate me, and I was afraid of her. I wanted a mom who was different, yet everyone else seemed to adore her humor and wit, love her beauty and charm.

Why had she hated only me?

Now she says, "I see why you couldn't look at me." Imagine thinking that your daughter couldn't look at you and not knowing why. That breaks my heart in two.

Now that we, my sister and I, are talking to her, truthfully; now that we have broken this vow of silence and someone else's shame; now that our perpetrator, dead since we were little, is dead of his control: now we are present with one another. The real brutality of that is that it is decades later. The stigma put upon us, by society, by its shameful lack of action, by secrets in families, in culture, in religions, in misogynistic realities everywhere, is out in the open. Yet we lost a lifetime of love, of our family.

Simply speaking this out loud to one another cleared the room, emptied the space between us, and let us see one another. I saw a woman I never really knew, a brilliant woman who never had a chance to dream, to imagine herself as any other thing, to imagine a life where she could be whatever she chose. She never had choices. No childhood, no parenting, no tenderness for her, no choices. Just make the best of what you get and be glad for it.

In her day a woman or girl could not or would not find solace or a place to go to speak and be safe. Her best safety was to be a child servant. This was her salvation. Her gift. In my day, my best was to try to protect my sister and then to go on to fight for the rights of those who had no voice, the abused, the unheard, those punished for simply being who they were born to be. Yet I could not and did not have a place to go to say who I was. An incest survivor.

Eventually I went to a twelve-step program for incest survivors, which I can highly recommend, as this is where I learned that this doesn't just happen to people who are losers and those who "have something wrong with them that attracts weirdos," as I had previously convinced myself by feeling so alone and damaged. No, in that room I saw judges and lawyers and people of extreme power, those who had chosen not to let people get away with such things, yet people who still had no one to tell about their own pain, and, worse, no one to listen.

We told, we listened. The friend I went with ended up dying by his own hand. He did not make it to this time, this brave time where we can and will say this out loud. We did not make it together, as my mother and my sister and I have.

Now, for the first time in my life, I understand just how much my mother loves me. When she told me that she taught me to "stand on your own two goddamn feet," that was her most loving and generous gift to me. That was the thing she had. The thing that she knew. The thing that helped her the most, the thing that saved her. That was the thing she knew for sure would be the most helpful to me and would save me time and time again. She was right. This world does not help women. It does not love women. It does not heal women, nor does it protect us. We must know how to stand on our own two goddamn feet, I am both proud and sorry to say. Only now I say it with all of the love I have, and I have so much. For now, I am able not only to receive love from my mother but to love my mother in return.

I don't need to know what she knew or blocked out to survive. I don't need to forgive her, or save her, or help her heal, or get her to help me. I am grateful that we both made it here. I respect her for that. She respects me for that. We can look each other in the eye.

If nothing else has come from this horrible time in our world now, of the most vulgar and oppositional things being said, let it be a time for all things *to* be said. Let us say this: this is a secret we will no longer keep. Sexual abuse in families is the nucleus of sexual abuse.

The decisions I made as an eight-year-old trying to protect both myself and my sister became not only a coping system but a way of life that I forgot to outgrow. Sometimes that was a good thing. I certainly didn't sleep my way into or around the business. But that didn't stop me from being sexually abused throughout my life, by people I knew and did not know, and by a lack of self-understanding. This has ended. Through education and compassion.

We must end it for everyone. Through governing, not shaming and public opinion. We need real laws for this: both felony
and misdemeanor laws. Rape kits must be processed, and men
must be taken seriously as victims.

We pretend that the numbers we read about are true when
they are not. We have shamed victims away from their honesty.
I want you to know the terrible mistakes and misfortunes that I
went through because of these poor antennae I had developed.
While I found amazing therapeutic ways through this, it took
so long for me to realize that this is what I was in therapy for!
Teachers, school systems, pediatricians all need much more
training. We must fund governmental studies to understand
and help children. It should be mandatory to create govern-
mentally funded, fully staffed options where it is safe for children to say what is happening to them in their homes. The
over-bright, underconfident child, the child trying too hard to
please, the introvert, the class clown, the bully, not just the bul-
lied, the bruised or battered—oh, gym teachers, pay attention!

No one came to help my grandmother. Her husband beat her
until the day he died. No one came to help my mother's sisters.

At sixteen, my mother became pregnant with my brother
and married my dad, at twenty-three giving birth to me, never,
ever having had a real day of childhood.

She was jealous of mine. It is easy to see why. She was still
a child when she had me and her terrible, strange youth was,
compared to the beautiful life she was working so hard to make
for us . . . gone.

My mother went back to school and graduated with my high

school class in 1975—and for her this was something. It is, as she says, what she did for "self-esteem." Yet, now that I know her and see her fully, I can only imagine for her who she truly could have been, what she could have done. Yet maybe this is it: she is and can be the torch that carries the light for women of her generation who are no longer afraid to stand up and be counted, to say, "No one will ever be abusive to me or anyone else again as long as I have a breath left in my body." For my mother, maybe now, her destiny is just beginning. As His Holiness the Dalai Lama said to me once, "A tiger does not apologize."

Today, my mother and I are at the beginning of our relationship. If I hadn't finally stopped keeping this horrible secret, I would never have known her. Never have understood her and certainly never have had the opportunity for her to mother me now that I've entered my sixties and my mother is in her mid-eighties.

One recent summer, when I was visiting my sister, we were all together for a few afternoons. We played cards, we laughed our brains out, I teased my mother about my childhood, about how she had ignored me. We laughed and cried. As I walked my mom to her car and buckled her into her seat, she said, "Next visit, why don't you come and stay with me?" I don't know if you can imagine what that means to me.

If only we could know our parents when we are children. If only our parents had been able to talk to us as we now are able to talk to our children. Because it feels like something has shifted culturally, and we can talk to our children and tell them about our childhoods. The good and the awful. We can tell them we have never been parents before, that this is our first time. We can say we don't know for sure what to do in a crisis, or when they do something wrong. We can say that we are struggling. It helps them to know that we are only human and doing the best that we can. They aren't stupid—they are just young. They aren't as naïve as you might imagine.

In fact, I am shocked by the things my boys teach me. Well, let's be frank: I have three adolescent boys. I am shocked by today's world. But I am so grateful that they are talking to me and I don't want them to stop, so I try not to seem too shocked. Even though they laugh at me.

And now, their grandma is skinning them at gin.

The Beauty of Living Twice

When I was in fifth grade, I struggled so much with my geography teacher. Geography was hard to grasp. Like many, if not most, of my classmates, I had never been anywhere—not even to Pittsburgh, which was ninety huge miles away. Even more significant, none of us thought we ever would go anywhere. Why would we?

But then, even then, somehow I wasn't buying it. Somehow, deep inside, I just didn't believe in the system. I questioned. I disagreed. I brought other books, proof of different thoughts, other ideas. I got a D for the first time. I was a straight-A student who got a D. Oh, I tried, I stayed up late, wrote a twenty-six-page extra paper that I offered up as a mea culpa, but my teacher, without even looking at it, threw it directly into the trash. No, no, there would be no thinking outside the box in Saegertown, Pennsylvania. Nope. The city limits were the limits of thought.

I cried myself to sleep for weeks. I guess my parents heard my inconsolable misery, for there were no punitive actions for this horrible crime of a D.

So again, I say, let's think outside the box. Let's think globally.

I have learned so much in Romania, Greece, Mexico, Puerto Rico, the Dominican Republic, the Caribbean, Canada, Norway, Denmark, Russia, Ukraine, Georgia, England, France, Italy, Poland, Austria, Switzerland, Belgium, South Africa, Zimbabwe, Uganda, Colombia, Brazil, Argentina, Spain, Morocco, Australia, Tahiti, Singapore, India, and China. These are the places that I can remember right now. All this travel has been astounding, jaw-dropping, humbling beyond all measure—and so completely outside of anything I ever expected. Me, the kid who got a D in geography, who was sure I would never go anywhere.

I wanted to, though: I wanted to see the world, to know how people thought and why, what mattered to them and why. It seems we care most about our loved ones. We want our kids to do well, better than we did. What that means differs from individual to individual, not country to country. Selfish people still want their children either to be just like them or to fulfill *their* unfulfilled dreams. Wounded people still want their children to be safe in that big, old, scary world that is far too dangerous to live in. Shut-down people don't know their kids. Warriors try to raise warriors, whether the kid is a wannabe warrior or not. Thus, the benefit of travel and open-mindedness: one can find one's own tribe.

I have seen the greatest beauty. The wonders of the world, and the wonders of my eye.

Watching the red sun rise in India is something of a miracle. You enter a dream state that does not end until you leave. The enchantment is complete. The smells, the tastes, the sounds of India. This only opens your senses so that you may fall into the colors. It is only then that the rituals and movements of the people become a song. At least for me. The bells, but not bells as we know them, not church bells, or school bells; no, the tinkling bells of ankle bracelets and hand bells, and bells on bikes and carts and doorways. The bells that signal the ends of sutras or the opening of thought.

The colors of the deserts. Deserts all over the world ignite a sense of mystery in me. The boys and I camped out in Morocco. We helicoptered out of the city to a stucco, very modern, but very Moorish-style hotel. I had never been anywhere or seen anything like this type of luxury: five-star Moorish luxury in the middle of seemingly nowhere. The food was fabulous, the people beautiful. We left the next a.m. to helicopter again for a couple of hours far out into the desert. The trip was jaw-dropping; we all had headphones and could talk to one another and the captain. We flew over hundreds of miles of desert. As we fell into the mesmerizing landscape, we began to see something up ahead—or was it a mirage?

The captain flew a bit lower but not low enough to disturb the sand dunes. They were a deep tan color and looked like waves of a soft, endless beige sea. We began to see what looked like a small camp; then we could make out that there were a few large tents, and some men in long robes with their heads covered. When we landed, we just started to run. We ran in the sand. We ran to the dunes. We rolled in the sand and rolled down the dunes.

Suddenly, one of the men dragged over a red-and-black rug and showed the boys how to carpet-surf the dunes. The boys wrapped their heads and covered their faces and ears to keep the sand out. My little Bedouins! I told them not to go more than two dunes away—it could be easy to lose their way back in this sea, which was now turning a distinctive shade of bright gold as far as the eye could see. We had dinner in our tent as it became dark, then walked to the top of the dune in front of our campsite and sat up there having mint tea and cookies.

The boys have now been to several far-flung places. Our last trip was to Alaska with my brother Pat; his wife, Tasha; and their kids, Kaylee and Hunter. I wanted us to see what was left. We saw icebergs actually break off in huge pieces and fall into the water, big pieces floating by everywhere, seals just looking at us helplessly as their homes were breaking down and melting into the water.

My brother caught a big salmon when he was fishing, and a bear came running up the side of the stream, as if to say, "Hey, what are you doing?" I think Patrick was both thrilled and taken aback. He threw the salmon back into the water. He did, however, catch another big boy a few days later, off the boat farther out, and on his birthday-party day.

We all learned a lot without using a lot of words. We didn't try to lecture the kids. We knew when they got back to school a lot of questions would come up. We knew they were now old enough to understand and reflect on what they saw. They missed about three days of school to do this trip, but I felt that they would learn more in those three days, things that would stay with them forever, than they might if they had stayed in school. I also felt that with the idea being tossed around that there is no global warming, I wanted them to see it for themselves so that they can make a valid argument on their own. I want them to know. To see, to understand.

Understanding comes in many ways. Like the first time I met Patti Smith, and I am bragging, it was in a restaurant in downtown New York City. I went in for a late lunch by myself and she was the only other person there, at a table by herself near the door. About six or seven minutes later, Donna Karan came in—still more bragging, by the way—and breezed by my table and sat far deeper into the joint, also alone. We all worked, ate, and kinda pretended that we weren't absorbing the others' loose molecules and feeling the edges of the others' worlds.

As I was having a cup of tea and reading something, Donna got up and strode across the room toward me, her fabulous coat blowing out behind her like the duster of the good cowboy at high noon. I was awestruck as she stopped to say hi. We talked for a few minutes and then Patti said, "Hey, I want in on this," her rough and smooth voice coming out of her leathers and that hair. Donna and I both looked up as the legend stood; I stood; it was like *Mick who????* There she was, and, well, Donna and I were starstruck. We all talked for a bit and traded details and left that place empty but for the dazzling enterprise of whoever arranges that kind of thing. God bless her fairy godmotherness.

From then on it seemed I ran into Patti kind of like you run into your guides. There she was in Paris raising money for Jude

Law to get the most difficult and dangerous people in the most difficult and dangerous war zones to for one day put down their weapons and get all of their kids vaccinated. It's called Peace One Day, and Jude puts on a full flak suit and walks up and down the most dangerous streets in the world to get this done. And there's Patti, and I say as I walk by, "Hey, Patti, somebody wants me to sing the songs that I write." She is onstage and I'm passing by to go rehearse introducing someone. Patti yells down, "You can do it, baby—I could only sing three notes when I started."

Yeah, so I go to rehearsal and get ready to do the show and Patti says she is going to take me onstage with her and I laugh. *Sure,* I think, *sure.* But I've seen this shit go down before— remind me to tell you about James Brown. All right, so I introduce a cool foreign band and it's all good, and then suddenly Patti and her band are up and I am retreating into the wings when Patti pulls me onto the stage behind the band and there I stand . . . the entire show. Just watching Patti f-ing Smith sing and thinking about her life. Her beautiful, interesting life; her photographs; Robert Mapplethorpe's unbelievable gifts; their friendship, *that friendship*—transcendent, that. I watch her sing, I cry a little bit; I see her beauty, her guts, her talent, that poetry; and before I know it people are cheering, she is bowing, and she grabs me and throws all of that energy around me and says, "Do you feel that, do you feel that, take that in, you get that, babe, I know you do, you do that, you can do this." And she walks off the stage, leaving me there to contemplate just what I can and cannot do.

Recently I worked with Meryl Streep, and I did not see that coming. We had side-eyed each other for at least two or three decades. I thought she was so very fancy, so far away from anyone I would understand or anyone who would ever see me. I thought this woman, this star, would never take the time to see little me. I saw her, I thought; I saw all of it, the Meryl Streep of it all.

Then I went to work with her, just for one day, on Steven Soderbergh's *The Laundromat,* and the most astounding thing happened. I met this woman who has four kids; I have three. She was about to be a grandmother and I was just so happy for her; I mean, God, a grandmother! We have been in this goddang business so long, and for a woman that is like dog years. Her daughters are actresses, all of them, and I want my son to learn how to use the camera. She is so clever, and interesting, and a person who I would choose as a friend if I met her at book club. How would we have ever known? The world has put women so at other ends of the room from one another. Put us at places where our first thing is to check ourselves at the door. My generation of women was still so tight-lipped, still so demure, still so careful. It could all be taken from us so quickly, we were threatened so often.

I did feel it when Patti hugged me. I felt the power of being myself in front of an audience and I know that she meant that this was enough for all of us. For her, for me—and I think both Meryl and I felt that with each other the other day. You know, this is more than a #MeToo thing; this is so big. We have to become safe with one another.

Yes, I can begin with the three notes I know, and I can stand on this stage and I can tell our story because I am unafraid to say it is our story. It is not the story of now, or the story of here, or the story of them. It is our story. It is the story of us, the story of women, and we are ready to sing a new story, and this now is how I am going to sing it. By telling you this.

It happened to me, to my sister, to my mother, to her mother, and to her mother before her. I am unashamed, I am unblemished, I am pure in my heart and in my soul, I am not bitter, I am not sad, I have no need to be washed clean, I am not angry, I am not here to punish you.

Your crimes belong to you. To you to own, to understand, to repair, to know, to grieve, to repent, and to leave behind.

This is what I have. I have my house. My story, my truth, which will not be true for everyone who stood next to me. Time is changing what is true every day. It is no longer healthy to be unkind.

I have learned to forgive the unforgivable. My hope is that as I share my journey, you too will learn to do the same.

I learned how to see differently. I learned this from dying, from living, and from being what I've often been called: "The Last Living Movie Star." I bring that up because I came from the era before digital, the era of analog. This means that it wasn't a computer projection you were seeing on the screen, it was seventy-millimeter or thirty-five, sometimes others, but what they had that digital doesn't is this. I'm letting you in on my secret, what I think made me a star.

I knew that the movie theater was special. It was for me: it was a place of wonder and magic, it was where you went to escape, to fall in love, to feel better, to learn, to grow, to find heroes and villains, and to hold hands with someone you were too afraid to reach for somewhere else. It was a place you could put your head on someone's shoulder and just be safe.

Why did that happen at the movies, then? Why did that help me become a star? Because I knew and played to that special thing. Sprockets. You see, analog film was strips of film with holes on the side and there was light that went through those holes. There was light that bled through, and every little bit on the screen wasn't a picture; sometimes some little microseconds were only light. It wasn't just the flat, nonstop drumming of pictures, so you could always see the theater and everyone in it—the flaws, the dirt, the empty food containers, the reality of it all. You could be alone in the dark and be immersed in the light. The tiny bits of glowing white light that would surround you, just you, and hypnotize you into that place that lets you rest, lets you feel free to trust your inner voice and love. That voice that lets you reach out and touch someone's hand, touch their heart, and share this experience—not get antsy and walk around the room, pause it when it got too much, and get some food, pee, and come back. No, honey, you held that and held on to yourself and them and couldn't wait to see what would happen next. Slow movies were engaging because you had each other and the thrill of the slowness, of the vibration of light and love.

I played to that. To the thrill, to the energy of that vibration. I loved that. As I kid, I lived for that. I saw that in black and white when it blew out places in those films. That was my avatar. That *is* my avatar, but now I know why.

We can reach for that light; we can look into that light. We can carry that light, be that light, and know that we are not digital, we cannot be replaced by that because we are the one thing that matters more. Call it what makes your heart sing; but call it with love, because that light will lift you, cleanse you, and save you. It is the beauty of living twice.

Acknowledgments

I would like to thank the many friends and family who read and listened to oh so many drafts of this book. I appreciate your candor and your love. First and foremost, my mother, Dorothy, who gave so much of herself to this, and my sister, Kelly, who so courageously allowed me to share a piece of her story. My brothers and friends who are in here—it's because I love you. My children, all three of them, were in my heart each day and night as I chose how to honor you by being my most truthful. Thank you, Roan, Laird, and Quinn. My brother-in-law, Bruce, has been a guiding light and an anchor for all of us.

None of this would have happened without the kindness of J. Kael Weston, one of the bravest and most decent men alive. Kael is an extraordinary writer who wrote about his experiences during the war in Afghanistan in his book, *The Mirror Test*. He and I met and became friends at Mary Haft's Nantucket Book Festival. I moved in with Mary and fell deeply in friendship with both of them. I started writing this as a book then and there in Mary's living room with their encouragement, poking, and prodding. They are the foundation on which this book stands.

Kael introduced me to Tim O'Connell, a masterly editor, no doubt. He brought the lovely and gifted Anna Kaufman on board and together they quite frankly taught me how to write a book. I often wrote while they pieced it all together. Sitting at Knopf in a room that had been occupied by far greater talents than I while writing and learning with these two extraordinarily gifted editors gave me courage and strength when I was unsure how to proceed. I owe this book to them in its entirety.

When the late Sonny Mehta, former head of Knopf, agreed to accept me as an author, I was honored by his talent, his history and knowledge, and his incredible understanding that there are many types of authors. Sonny encouraged me: "You are my next Irish storyteller." He made me want to be better than I thought I knew how.

There isn't enough thanks to say what it means to start putting a book together in the company of legitimate authors, those brave people who have already bared their souls and who stood beside me believing that I could do the same. I respect and admire you greatly.

I always thought that Joan Didion was the greatest writer and I read and reread her work while I wrote this. God bless you, Ms. Didion.

Then there is the legal work of Dan Novack and the PR work of Paul Bogaards, or "Bogie," which were thorough and joyfully done. I appreciate that so much; it is a pleasure and a joy to work with you. Thank you to Amy Edelman and Amy Brosey for their diligent copy edits, as well as to Reagan Arthur, Maya Mavjee, Kathy Hourigan, Maria Massey, Suzanne Smith, Serena Lehman, John Gall, Andy Hughes, Kristen Bearse, Sean Yule, and everyone else at Knopf for helping along the way. And to my literary agent, Luke Janklow, of Janklow and Nesbit, for his guidance.

I would like to thank the women in my office, Tina Manning and Sandra Tello, who printed and struck so many pages. Tina, especially, listened to so much of this that she will never need to read it!

While this book is but a bit of a full and complex life it is the bit that I needed to find so that I may make sense of the rest.

I am writing my thanks during a long quarantine period for all of us, and my gratitude comes with clarity and consciousness. I have found a great deal of peace from this process, something that has given me an opportunity to find something new in me during this very unusual and complex time in the world. So, in advance, I thank you, the reader, for sharing in this experience, and wish you some of the same clarity that I have found.

There are real names and aliases in this book, not because I love some people more or less, but simply out of respect for their privacy; some asked for this, some didn't. Some people were left out, not because I don't think of you but because this piece of my life wasn't about us. Next time perhaps.

I suppose it may seem silly to some, but my dogs by my side late into the night and early in the morning while I cried and wrote, who sit by me now, gave me a solace that is ongoing and dear to me.

Last, I want to thank my ex-husband Phil, and his new wife, Chris, for finding a path to a whole, healthy, and blending family with me. There is no greater gift.

Resource Guide

If you or someone you love has experienced sexual or domestic violence and are seeking help, these organizations have excellent resources and support staff, most available 24/7.

loveisrespect
866-331-9474
TTY 800-787-3224
Text LOVEIS to 22522
www.loveisrespect.org

Planned Parenthood
800-230-7526
Text PPNOW to 774636
www.plannedparenthood.org

National Domestic Violence Hotline
800-799-SAFE or 800-799-7233
TTY 800-787-3224
www.thehotline.org

RAINN (Rape, Abuse & Incest National Network) and the
National Sexual Assault Hotline
800-656-HOPE or 800-656-4673
www.rainn.org

Stop It Now!
1-888-PREVENT
Helpline hours are Monday–Friday 12 p.m. to 6 p.m. EST
www.stopitnow.org

Survivors of Incest Anonymous
877-SIA-WSO1 or 877-742-9761
www.siawso.org

TEEN LINE
800-852-8336
Text TEEN to 839863
www.teenlineonline.org